# Instant Family Devotions

## Also by Mike Nappa

*Instant Small Group*

*The Jesus Survey*

# Instant Family Devotions

## 52 Bible Discussions for Anytime, Anywhere Use

Mike Nappa and
Jill Wuellner

BakerBooks
a division of Baker Publishing Group
Grand Rapids, Michigan

Published by Baker Books
a division of Baker Publishing Group
P.O. Box 6287, Grand Rapids, MI 49516-6287
www.bakerbooks.com

Printed in the United States of America



Library of Congress Cataloging-in-Publication Data
Nappa, Mike, 1963–
Instant family devotions : 52 Bible discussions for anytime, anywhere use / Mike Nappa and Jill Wuellner.
p. cm.
Includes bibliographical references (p. ) and indexes.
ISBN 978-0-8010-1433-8 (pbk.)
1. Families—Prayers and devotions. I. Wuellner, Jill. II. Title.
BV255.N39 2012
249—dc22 2012000775



This book is published in association with Nappaland Literary Agency, an independent agency dedicated to publishing works that are: Authentic. Relevant. Eternal. Visit us on the web at: NappalandLiterary.com



12 13 14 15 16 17 18 7 6 5 4 3 2 1

In keeping with biblical principles of creation stewardship, Baker Publishing Group advocates the responsible use of our natural resources. As a member of the Green Press Initiative, our company uses recycled paper when possible. The text paper of this book is composed in part of post-consumer waste.

We feed children in order that they may soon be able to feed themselves; we teach them in order that they may soon not need our teaching.

—C. S. Lewis[1]

# Contents

# Introduction

## *Who Is Watty Piper Anyway?*

The interesting thing, really, is that Watty Piper doesn't even exist.

Still, if you're like many American families, Mr. Piper has had the most significant faith conversation with your children since their preschool days—despite his status of nonbeing.

You see, our dear Watty Piper is the pseudonym some enterprising editor at Platt & Munk Publishers dreamed up in 1930 to use as the byline for a children's picture book. The story in that little tome had been around for decades, told in one form or another as a folktale for kids. When Platt & Munk decided to retell it during the Great Depression, it resonated with the can-do spirit of America and became an immediate classic. Some eighty-plus years later, it's still a staple in most family libraries, nurseries, and daycare centers.

So what did Watty Piper write? We'll give you a hint:

*I think I can, I think I can . . .*

Yep, Watty Piper is the fictional author of *The Little Engine That Could*.

This is the story of a small roundhouse utility engine that dares to accomplish what everyone else thought was impossible: singlehandedly pulling a long chain of railcars up a steep hillside. Chances are very good that you read this book—repeatedly—to your own children. And if you didn't, one of their teachers or babysitters or librarians or aunts or uncles did.

In fact, that Little Engine recently ranked in the top half (number thirty-one, to be exact) of *The 101 Most Influential People Who Never Lived*. The authors of this list describe the Little Engine's impact this way: "She chants to herself as she pulls, repeating her belief in her own ability, perhaps the first mantra of positive thinking. . . . She teaches us that we should believe in ourselves, to believe that we *can* do it."[1]

Now, *The Little Engine That Could* is a fine, inspiring storybook . . . *unless* it's the only place where faith conversations happen in your kids' lives. Unlike a little engine, in real life we can't simply believe in ourselves and hope that's enough. True faith must be grounded in God alone—and only then can we accomplish great things.

Likewise, most of the books and television shows and radio programs and iPod playlists and DVR lineups and movies and more that your kids consume are fine forms of entertainment for your kids . . . *unless* they're shaping your family members' beliefs without the benefit of a rich tradition of family faith conversations to go along with them.

And that's why *Instant Family Devotions* exists.

No, we're not suggesting that you burn all copies of *The Little Engine That Could*, or saying you should smash your television set or check out from American culture and literature. That's absurd. But we are saying that talking about faith in the context of American family culture is important and influences both the here and the hereafter.

And so, *Instant Family Devotions* was created to help your family do just that. To help you and your kids add a few fun, faith-building conversations to your twenty-first-century lifestyle. To help you take charge of the faith-growth opportunities that come during the raising of a child. To help you join the ongoing conversation about God that goes on every day in your child's mind and life. To help you be ready—anytime, anywhere—with a few creative, Bible-centered family devotions to share with your kids. To give you an easy-to-use tool for making fun, family faith memories that'll last a lifetime.

It's that simple . . . and that easy . . . and that powerful.

What's more, this book really is as "instant" as the title suggests. The devotions in here require zero prep, meaning you and your kids can literally open this book and *go*. That means family faith conversations can happen:

- Around the dinner table
- On a car trip
- Hanging out at a park or at the beach
- When you're stuck inside on a wintry day
- In an airport
- During family nights and get-togethers
- When you're hanging out in the living room
- On the carpool ride home from school
- Just before bedtime
- Anytime!

And hey, there's more than just that at your disposal in here. We've also included "Behind the Scenes" Bible background boxes so you and your family can get a sense of the context of a chosen passage of Scripture. And we went ahead and threw in a bunch of optional, simple add-ons you can try (just for fun) with the devotions.

So there it is.

When you share the faith conversations in this book with your kids, you all grow closer to God—and to each other. Exploring the Bible with these devotions encourages critical thinking and builds a foundation of deep family faith. And honestly, with *Instant Family Devotions*, leading a Bible exploration with your kids has never been easier, or more fun.

So go ahead and jumpstart your family's faith. Take a deep breath. Say a quick prayer. Gather your kids. Say to yourself, *I think God can, I think God can.* Then turn the page and get growing today.

Have fun!

Mike Nappa & Jill Wuellner
2012

# How to Use This Book

Wow, you're such a cool parent.

You're about to lead your kids into an unforgettable adventure in God's Word! And don't worry; *Instant Family Devotions* will give you everything you need to do just that.

Here's what you need to know before you begin.

## What Kind of Families Use This Book?

*Instant Family Devotions* is designed to work best with families that have at least one parent present and upper elementary to high school-aged children. Generally, if your kids are readers, they'll enjoy these devotions—and grow in a relationship with Christ as a result.

With that said, however, if you have children who are younger or older, say preschool or college-aged, don't assume this book is off-limits to them. For preschoolers, an older child or a parent can often help bridge the conversation (and read the Bible passages) for them. College and career-aged kids can help take the conversation deeper, and often will challenge their younger siblings to think—especially if they are the ones leading the devotion. Which brings us to the next question . . .

## Who Leads an Instant Family Devotion?

At the beginning, we'd recommend that a parent lead until the kids get comfortable with the process and their levels of participation. But, honestly, anyone who can read can lead one of these family devotions—they're that flexible.

After a few weeks, feel free to hand off this book to one of your children and have that person lead the family in devotion time. There's no prep required, so he or she can just open the book and go—and your child will gain greater insights and practice at leading others in talking about God. All good things, right?

## How Often Should We Have a Family Devotion?

There are fifty-two devotions in this book, and we're kind of assuming that means you'll use one each week for a year. Of course, you don't have to do that. During summer, you may want to have family devotions two or three times a week, for instance. Or during a busy Christmas season, you may need to skip a week or two.

Really, you can use these anytime or anywhere, so feel free to set the schedule that works for your family, then relax and enjoy. The important thing is not so much *when* you have family devotions, but that you *do* have family devotions.

## What Kind of Prep Work Is Needed to Pull Off One of These Family Devotions?

Hmmm . . . Let's see.

First, open this book to any discussion guide.

Then, go.

## Seriously? That's All It Takes?

Yep. Leading a family devotion has never been so easy.

Other than a Bible, there are no supplies required. And because each discussion guide includes relevant info for you about cultural and textual interpretation of the Bible, no pre-lesson prep is needed either. That way you can discover God's Word together with your kids in fresh, interactive, discussion-starting ways.

The "Behind the Scenes" boxes are primarily for you, the parent, but can also be shared with your kids. However, they include word studies, historical insights, commentary notes, and more, so they may be a bit heavy for younger children. Use the insights here to inform your own understanding of Scripture, and to help you as you guide your family discussions. If your kids are older and more inquisitive, feel free to share these "Behind the Scenes" bits with them if they're interested, but don't feel obligated to do so if it doesn't seem appropriate for their maturity level.

If you want to do more during a devotion, or if you have access to simple supplies (such as paper and pencils), we've frequently included special "Parent Tip: For Extra Fun" boxes with advice for adding extra elements to a discussion. But really, these add-ons are not required for your devotion experience. All you need is this book and a Bible. Oh, and your kids, of course.

## How Long Is an Instant Family Devotion?

Each devotion in this book runs between thirty and fifty minutes, depending on your family's discussion habits.

## What Happens During a Devotion?

Each discussion guide in this book follows the same structure.

**OPEN UP**

This is a fun, lighthearted opening question or two to introduce the theme of the session and to help your family members learn a little bit more about each other.

**OPEN BOOK**

This is the heart of the devotion. It's where you dig into Scripture, ask the hard questions, and begin to explore how the messages of the Bible relate to your family members' real lives.

**OPEN LIFE**

Here's where you'll both challenge and encourage your family members to take what they've learned so far and let it show up in their lives during the coming week.

## What about Others? Can They Join in the Devotion?

Well, sure!

If your kids want to include their friends in your family devotion, the more the merrier. Or if you've got relatives over for the weekend, they can join in too. The devotions here are flexible and inviting, so feel free to include anyone who happens to be around when you start.

If you want to adapt this book and use it with a multi-family group (say, in a small group study, or a multi-age Sunday school class, or on a retreat), you can do that too. You and your kids can also choose to work through these discussion guides individually, as a private devotion or Scripture study time. You really can use this book anytime, anywhere, and with anyone (or with no one else at all!).

## Anything Else I Should Know?

Let's see . . .

Jesus cares about you, your spouse, your kids, and your *family*—even more than you do. And using this book to discover more of God's Word, the Bible, will change *everyone* (including you).

So, you know, be ready for that—it's kind of exciting to watch it happen.

May God bless you and your family!

SECTION 1

# Discussion Guides about the Old Testament

# 1

# Picture Perfect

God said, "Let us make mankind in our image."
Genesis 1:26

THEME: **Created in God's Image**
SCRIPTURE: **Genesis 1:26–31**

## OPEN UP

1. Look around at each person in our family. If someone hadn't met us before, how would they know we're all related? Give examples.

2. People don't have to look like twins for others to see a family resemblance. What other clues tell that we're family? For instance, the ways we act, the things we think are funny, or the things we do?

**Parent Tip:** For Extra Fun

If you like, pull out a few family photo albums and thumb through them as you explore answers to questions 1 and 2. Or have all your family members crowd in front of a bathroom mirror while you chat!

OPEN BOOK

3. Why do you suppose family members tend to be similar to each other, both in looks and in personality?

***Have family members read Genesis 1:26–31.***

4. When God created people, he did more than just welcome us into his family—he actually made people "in his image." What do you think that means?

5. Up to this point, when God was creating the world and animals and things, he said his creation was "good." When he created humans, he said it was "*very* good" (see v. 31). Why do you think he said that?

**Behind the Scenes:** Genesis 1:26

The Hebrew word translated as "image" in this Scripture is *tselem*.

While "resemblance" is the clearest meaning of *tselem*, it also carries with it the figurative impression of shade or a shadow, as though God cast his shadow on us during creation and left it there.[1] One significant implication of that concept lies in the nature of a shadow itself: in order for it to be cast, what it represents *must* be nearby.

Thus, God's constant image *in* us is also the comfort of God's constant nearness *to* us.

6. What do people say or do that shows God's family resemblance in their lives? Give examples.

7. If you could ask God anything about the way he created people, what would you ask? Why?

8. How do you think God would answer those questions?

## OPEN LIFE

9. How does it make you feel to know that God miraculously made you to be like him? Explain.

10. If you could give God a compliment about the way he created people, what would you say? Let's pray those compliments right now!

**Parent Tip**

Encourage family members to be specific in the way they answer "Open Life" questions. Also, instruct kids to wait a minute or two in silence before answering. This will give them an opportunity to think through their responses a bit before having to talk about them.

# 2

# Tip-Top Tower

The Lord scattered them from there over all the earth, and they stopped building.

Genesis 11:8

THEME: **Pride**
SCRIPTURE: **Genesis 11:1–9**

## OPEN UP

1. Poof! You've been granted three wishes (and one of them can't be for additional wishes). What will you wish for?
2. If one of your wishes was to instantly be able to speak any foreign language, which language would you want it to be? Why?

**Parent Tip:** For Extra Fun

If you have it, pull out your family's Jenga game and play during or before this discussion time. It'll add a nice visual to accompany the conversation.

## OPEN BOOK

3. Imagine you woke up tomorrow morning and everyone around you spoke a foreign language. What would you feel like? What would you do?

***Have family members read Genesis 11:1–9.***

4. What's your first reaction when you hear this story?
5. Genesis 11:4 says the people wanted to "make a name for themselves." Why was this a problem, from God's view?

**Behind the Scenes:** Genesis 11:4

The tower in Genesis 11:4 was likely a *ziggurat*—a large temple dedicated to a specific pagan god. Similar in appearance to an Egyptian pyramid, this tower would have been square at the bottom. Each outside "wall" would have been made up of long rows of stairs leading up and in toward a small shrine at the top.[2]

Interestingly, the people here wanted to build this tower to "make a name" for themselves worldwide. They succeeded, but not in the way they planned. Instead of being celebrated and revered for their architectural achievement, they've gone down in history as arrogant fools easily humbled by our almighty God.[3]

6. In this passage we see that God is interested in what we do as well as our character and our inner motivation. How does this make you feel about God? Explain.
7. By today's standards, building a tower doesn't seem like such a big deal. Why do you think God acted in such an extreme way toward the Tower of Babel, but does not act the same toward us when we build tall towers today?
8. The Bible makes it clear that God dislikes prideful, self-centered attitudes. Why do you think this is?

## OPEN LIFE

9. Based on what you read in Genesis 11, what do you think is God's definition of success?

10. What tips can we learn from this story to help us have God's attitude toward success this week?

**Parent Tip**

Encourage family members to be specific in the way they answer "Open Life" questions. Also, allow kids to wait a minute or two in silence before answering. This will give them an opportunity to think through their responses a bit before having to talk about them.

# 3

# Introducing . . .

Surely the LORD is in this place, and I was not aware of it.
Genesis 28:16

THEME: **Meeting God**
SCRIPTURE: **Genesis 28:10–22**

## OPEN UP

1. Are you an early bird or night owl? Why?
2. Admit it: whether it's a teddy bear or a favorite pillow, we all have something we need to help us sleep soundly. What helps you get a good night's sleep?

**Parent Tip:** For Extra Fun

Use fabric markers to decorate pillowcases that family members can keep as reminders of what they learned in today's discussion!

**OPEN BOOK**

3. With rocks under your sleeping bag or scrunched up in the car or something else . . . where's the most uncomfortable place you've ever slept?

***Have family members read Genesis 28:10–22.***

4. Jacob slept on a rock (ouch!) and dreamed of heaven. What was it about this vision that made him take it seriously and not simply brush it off as just a strange dream?

5. After meeting God in this dream, Jacob was in awe and afraid. How do you think you might feel if you were to meet God in your dreams tonight? Describe it.

**Behind the Scenes:** Genesis 28:12, 19

Jacob's experience in Genesis 28 is the first time recorded in Scripture that God used a dream to communicate with a man. Prior to that, God had appeared in person to both Jacob's father Isaac and his grandfather Abraham.

After this dream, Jacob renamed the place where it occurred. It had been known as *Luz* (meaning "light"), but Jacob gave it new honor by calling it *Bethel* (meaning "house of God"). Centuries later, so many people there had turned away from God that the prophet Hosea actually condemned this place with the name *Beth Aven*, meaning "house of idols" (Hosea 4:15). Although no longer the same city, this place is now home to the village of Beitin in the West Bank of Palestine.[4]

6. Jacob set his rock as a memorial of sorts to commemorate his meeting with God. Why is it important to remember when God is active in our lives?

7. Tell about a time when you "met" or saw God working in your life. What do you remember about that?

8. What if Jacob came to our house for dinner? What do you think he might tell us about meeting God in his sleep?

## OPEN LIFE

9. Jacob named the place where he slept in honor of God. What name could you give your bedroom that would honor God? Explain your choice.

10. How can we help each other look for God's presence in our lives each day this week?

**Parent Tip**

Encourage family members to be specific in the way they answer "Open Life" questions. Also, allow kids to wait a minute or two in silence before answering. This will give them an opportunity to think through their responses a bit before having to talk about them.

# 4

# Ten to Win

And God spoke all these words.
Exodus 20:1

THEME: **Ten Commandments**
SCRIPTURE: **Exodus 20:1–17**

## OPEN UP

1. Time to find out if you've been listening all these years! What are the rules of our family, as you understand them?
2. If you could make up one new rule our family had to live by, what would it be?

**Parent Tip:** For Extra Fun

Why not redecorate your living room (move furniture, add posters, etc.) to resemble a courtroom for this devotion? Add a long robe, and you and your family members can take turns being the "judge" who asks each new discussion question!

OPEN BOOK

***Have family members read Exodus 20:1–17.***

3. Why do you think God gave us these "family rules" for life? Explain.

4. Let's think about how this works. For instance, when you're at school, what does it mean not to "have any other gods" except God? What about when you're at home?

5. God gave us reasons for following some of these Ten Commandments (see vv. 4–12), but for others he gave no reason at all (see vv. 13–17). Why do you think he did that?

**Behind the Scenes:** Exodus 20:1–17

The Ten Commandments recorded in Exodus are probably the most famous part of Scripture. Scholars call these commands "The Decalogue," while in Hebrew they are known as simply "The Ten Words." In the ancient Hebrew form, these commands are actually ten brief statements of only two words each.[5]

The Ten Words here fall into only two categories: (1) instructions regarding our relationship with God (commandments 1–4), and (2) instructions regarding our relationship with others (commandments 5–10). Those categories mirror exactly what Jesus identified as the two greatest commandments in Matthew 22:37–39: (1) love the Lord, and (2) love your neighbor.[6]

6. Look at verse 12. What does it really mean to "honor your father and mother"? Give examples.

7. How would your friendships change if everyone ignored God's Ten Commandments? Describe it.

8. A lot of time passed between the time of Adam and Eve and when God gave people the Ten Commandments. Why do you think God waited so long to share these laws?

## OPEN LIFE

9. The Ten Commandments can be seen as just a list of rules, but they also reveal a lot about God's personality and what he thinks is important. What do you notice about God just from reading Exodus 20:1–17?

10. What can we gain from following God's "family rules" in our home this week? At school? Anywhere?

**Parent Tip**

Encourage family members to be specific in the way they answer "Open Life" questions. Also, allow kids to wait a minute or two in silence before answering. This will give them an opportunity to think through their responses a bit before having to talk about them.

# 5

# Donkey Sermons

Your path is a reckless one.
Numbers 22:32

THEME: **Perspective**
SCRIPTURE: **Numbers 22:21–35**

## OPEN UP

1. Rumor has it that the animals of the world are keeping track of the ways we humans live and act. If the household pets in our neighborhood were to give a report about us, what do you think they'd say?

2. How would you respond if an animal suddenly spoke to you? Show us.

**Parent Tip:** For Extra Fun

If the circumstances are right, consider having this devotion during a trip to the zoo or another place where animals are present.

## OPEN BOOK

***Have family members read Numbers 22:21–35.***

3. From Balaam's perspective, his donkey's antics had embarrassed him in front of the important princes of Moab. That made him so mad he wasn't even surprised by a donkey talking! What do you think was going through his mind at that moment?

4. From God's perspective, he was angry that Balaam had been tempted to betray Israel in return for riches from the princes of Moab. Why do you think Balaam was unaware of God's perspective?

5. What keeps us from considering God's perspective in our daily lives (such as at school, at home, or when hanging out with friends)? Explain.

**Behind the Scenes:** Numbers 22:21–35

A prophet is defined as "a person authorized to speak for God."[7] As such, the prophet Balaam must have felt a certain amount of pride in knowing that he'd been chosen by God to speak the blessings and curses of heaven. This self-satisfaction was likely increased by the fact that the king of Moab was willing to pay princely sums for a single prophetic curse from Balaam's mouth.

Imagine how humbling it must have been for Balaam when God used a donkey to rebuke him! The implication must have been clear: as far as God was concerned, the great and mighty Balaam could easily be replaced by something as lowly as a brutish pack animal. Balaam apparently got the message (at least for a short time), and spoke a blessing on Israel instead of the curse he had been paid to say.

6. Balaam was known as God's prophet, someone who spoke for God. How do you think he felt when God used a lowly donkey to speak for him instead of Balaam?

7. Balaam let the promise of riches and his own inflated ego blind him to God's perspective. What advice do you have for Balaam and for others like him? Be specific.

8. To help Balaam see the mistakes he was making, God sent an angel to him and even made a donkey talk! What does God use today to help correct us when we're straying from what he wants for us?

## OPEN LIFE

9. If Balaam's donkey were here right now, what message from God do you think she'd speak to us? Why?

10. What can we do this week to help each other keep God's perspective in mind as we live out our lives? List three things.

**Parent Tip**

Encourage family members to be specific in the way they answer "Open Life" questions. Also, allow kids to wait a minute or two in silence before answering. This will give them an opportunity to think through their responses a bit before having to talk about them.

# 6

# Walls Come Tumblin'

At the sounds of the trumpet, when the men gave a loud shout, the wall collapsed.

Joshua 6:21

THEME: **Facing Challenges**
SCRIPTURE: **Joshua 6:1–25**

## OPEN UP

1. Would you rather climb the highest mountain, run the fastest mile, or swim across the ocean? Why?
2. What kinds of challenges would you have to face in order to do any of those three things?

**Parent Tip:** For Extra Fun

After this devotion, have a little family fun. Rearrange your furniture to create a (safe) obstacle course. Then take turns trying to get through it blindfolded. Be sure to shout like Joshua's soldiers when anyone is victorious!

## OPEN BOOK

*Have family members read Joshua 6:1–25.*

3. When it came to conquering Jericho, what challenges did the Israelites have to face? Let's make a list.
4. When it comes to living for God in our daily lives, what challenges do we sometimes have to face?
5. It seems odd that the Israelites were challenged to remain silent while they marched around the city (see v. 10). Do you find it easier or harder when a challenge seems odd? Explain.

**Behind the Scenes:** Joshua 6:1–25

The actual city of Jericho has been excavated by archaeologists for more than a hundred years. As Scripture indicates, there is barely anything left of the walls that once surrounded Jericho, and there is evidence that the city was destroyed by fire (as reported in Josh. 6:24). In spite of that, some people have tried to invent new explanations for how the city was destroyed, refusing to believe that God miraculously intervened on behalf of Joshua and the Israelites.

Some of the more popular (and occasionally silly) theories include:

a. The trumpets the Israelites blew were so loud that sound waves from them caused Jericho's walls to collapse.
b. The stomping feet of the soldiers walking around the city was enough to cause earthquake-like shock waves that knocked down the walls of Jericho.
c. The people of Jericho were so distracted by soldiers marching around their city all week they didn't notice other soldiers sneaking in and tearing out the base of the city walls.[8]

6. Imagine you are an Israelite at this time. *You hear the horn blow and Joshua commands everyone to yell as loudly as they can. You join the shouting, and then . . .* Tell what happens next! What are the sights and sounds that you experience?

7. The battle plan for Jericho was a little crazy, yet Joshua had complete trust in God to bring victory. Why?

8. Looking at what happened in Jericho, what part did obedience play in Joshua's victory?

## OPEN LIFE

9. What part does obedience play in helping you face challenges in life? (For instance, when you don't feel well, when your friends are mean, or when church seems confusing.) Explain what you mean.

10. What's one way you'd like to imitate Joshua this week? Why?

**Parent Tip**

Encourage family members to be specific in the way they answer "Open Life" questions. Also, allow kids to wait a minute or two in silence before answering. This will give them an opportunity to think through their responses a bit before having to talk about them.

# 7

# Me and My House

As for me and my household, we will serve the LORD.
Joshua 24:15

THEME: **Serving God**
SCRIPTURE: **Joshua 24:14–24**

## OPEN UP

1. Let's talk about choices. It's Saturday morning: Do you stay in bed and sleep late, or get up early and get to work on the day's chores?

2. How about this: you must choose between chocolate and caramel. How about pizza or steak? Time alone or time with friends? Church or television? Homework or class work? Now or tomorrow?

**Parent Tip:** For Extra Fun

When answering question 2, designate opposite sides of the room to represent each option. Then have kids move to the appropriate side to demonstrate their choices. See if anybody can be convinced to switch sides!

## OPEN BOOK

***Have family members read Joshua 24:14–24.***

3. According to Joshua, the Israelites had to make a choice: serve God or don't serve God. Why was that a hard decision for them?

4. Joshua 24:14 instructs people to "fear the Lord." What do you think that means?

5. When they remembered what God had done in their lives, it helped the people to choose God with confidence. If you were in the same situation, what could you remember about God to give you confidence?

**Behind the Scenes:** Joshua 24:14–24

During the time of Joshua, political treaties typically involved a suzerain (a powerful nation or king) and a vassal (a less-powerful nation or king). When peace agreements were made between these two nations, they typically followed a strict format: identification of the suzerain, along with his credentials and greatness; a little history of the relationship between the suzerain and vassal; a list of the obligations of each party; and instructions, witnesses, and consequences for violating the treaty. Usually, the suzerain promised peace and protection while the vassal promised loyalty. This type of political treaty would have been very familiar to Joshua and the people of Israel. Not surprisingly, it's the same format used in Joshua 24:14–24.

In short, Joshua 24:14–24 is the historic record of a cosmic peace treaty between God—our limitless, eternal suzerain—and both the nation of Israel and its individual citizens.[9]

6. What does it mean to serve God "with all faithfulness"?
7. Joshua actually made it kind of tough for the people to choose God. It's almost like he tried to talk them out of it. Why do you think he did that?
8. When it's hard for you to serve God, what keeps you committed to him?

## OPEN LIFE

9. If we said, like Joshua, "As for me and my house, we will serve the Lord," how would anybody know about it?
10. What are seven ways we can serve the Lord? Let's try to do one of those each day this week!

**Parent Tip**

Encourage family members to be specific in the way they answer "Open Life" questions. Also, allow kids to wait a minute or two in silence before answering. This will give them an opportunity to think through their responses a bit before having to talk about them.

# 8

# Too Easy for God!

The LORD said to Gideon, "You have too many men."
Judges 7:2

THEME: **Obedience**
SCRIPTURE: **Judges 7:1–22**

## OPEN UP

1. If you were the host of your own talk show, which celebrities would you want to have as guests during your first week on television? Why?

2. What kinds of questions would you want to ask those people? How do you think they might answer?

**Parent Tip:** For Extra Fun

If you're doing this at your home, pretend your living room is the set of a talk show (like *The Tonight Show* or *The Late Show*). Then conduct the devotion as a talk show interview, with you playing the role of the host and your family members playing the roles of the celebrity guests.

## OPEN BOOK

***Have family members read Judges 7:1–22.***

3. If a member of Gideon's army were a guest on your TV show, what kinds of questions would you want to ask him? How do you think he'd answer?

4. It must have been tough for Gideon to send away 32,000 soldiers and keep only three hundred—especially knowing that the Midianite army was such an overwhelming fighting force. What do you think helped him obey God even when it could have cost him his life?

5. When is it tough for you to obey God? What helps you do it anyway?

**Behind the Scenes:** Judges 7:5–6

Selecting soldiers based on the way they drink water is clearly an unusual method for putting together a fighting force. This command from God has puzzled theologians (and others) for centuries. The conventional thinking is that the three hundred men who "lapped" the water like dogs demonstrated that they were more alert, more skilled soldiers, capable of victory in battle. This, however, is inconsistent with God's purpose as described in Judges 7:2, in order that Israel may not boast, "My own strength has saved me."

Bible historian Stephen Miller offers a less glamorous but more realistic explanation: "This probably wasn't a test to find only the most alert fighters," he says, "since that could have been seen to reduce God's role in the battle. It was probably just a quick way of drastically cutting the size of the army."[10]

6. God allowed Gideon to see what was going on "behind the scenes" in the Midianite camp, and that encouraged

him to act with confidence. What do you think we'd see if God gave us a peek "behind the scenes" of our lives and our circumstances?

7. What might help us have confidence that God is at work in our lives even when we can't see "behind the scenes"? Let's make a list.

8. Gideon obeyed God and won a great victory. However, if God had allowed Gideon to be defeated, do you think that would have been a failure on Gideon's part? Defend your answer.

## OPEN LIFE

9. God allows both victory and defeat in our daily lives. What will you do about that? Explain.

10. If you were to pray, "Jesus, make me like Gideon" each day this week, how do you think God would answer? Want to try it and see what happens?

**Parent Tip**

Encourage family members to be specific in the way they answer "Open Life" questions. Also, allow kids to wait a minute or two in silence before answering. This will give them an opportunity to think through their responses a bit before having to talk about them.

# 9

# Faithful Friends

Where you go I will go.
Ruth 1:16

THEME: **Loyalty**
SCRIPTURE: **Ruth 1:3–18**

## OPEN UP

1. Adjectives, adjectives! Remember those beautiful, talented, meaningful describing words? Which of them would you use to describe yourself?

2. What adjectives would you use to describe our family as a whole? Why?

**Parent Tip:** For Extra Fun

For a twist, you might want to have family members brainstorm a list of twenty or more adjectives *before* asking them question 1.

Then you can have kids choose adjectives off the list in response to questions 1, 2, and 3.

## OPEN BOOK

***Have family members read Ruth 1:3–18.***

3. What adjectives would you use to describe Ruth?
4. Ruth could have remained in Moab with her family and friends. It couldn't have been easy to leave everything and everyone she ever knew. Why did she go to Bethlehem with Naomi?
5. Besides her words, what actions show you Ruth's loyal love for Naomi?

**Behind the Scenes:** Ruth 1:3–5

The death of Naomi's husband, and also of Ruth's husband, carried more than emotional significance in the male-dominated society where they lived. In that time, widows like Ruth and Naomi were at genuine risk of starvation or abuse. According to Bible historians, "Widows in the ancient Near East had lost all social status and generally were also without political or economic status. They would equate to the homeless in our American society."[11]

It would have taken great courage for Ruth to throw in her lot with her "homeless" mother-in-law—yet that's exactly what she did. And, surprisingly, we've benefited from that decision: Ruth ended up being an ancestor to Joseph, the stepfather of Jesus Christ.

6. What if Naomi came to our home for ice cream tonight? What would she tell us about her friendship with Ruth?
7. Would you want Ruth to be your friend? Why or why not?
8. If Ruth were your friend, and she came over for ice cream, what would she tell us about you?

## OPEN LIFE

9. Ruth is a great example of a loyal friend, but God is even more loyal than Ruth. How have you seen or experienced God's loyal love this past month?

10. What can we learn from Ruth's example to help us be loyal, loving people toward each other? Toward people outside our family?

**Parent Tip**

Encourage family members to be specific in the way they answer "Open Life" questions. Also, allow kids to wait a minute or two in silence before answering. This will give them an opportunity to think through their responses a bit before having to talk about them.

# 10

# Inside-Out Eyesight

The LORD looks at the heart.
1 Samuel 16:7

THEME: **Character/Inner Beauty**
SCRIPTURE: **1 Samuel 16:4–13**

## OPEN UP

1. Eyes, teeth, hair, clothes? What's the first thing you notice when you meet someone new?

2. If you could change anything about yourself, what would it be? Tell why.

**Parent Tip:** For Extra Fun

Before starting this devotion, use your cell phone or digital camera to take a quick picture of each family member. Let each person look at his or her picture when answering question 2.

OPEN BOOK

3. What would you say are the best things about the person next to you?

***Have family members read 1 Samuel 16:4–13.***

4. Samuel looked at Eliab and, based on his appearance, assumed he would be the best person to be king. What do you think Samuel saw in Eliab?

5. Eliab and his brothers weren't bad people, but God still rejected them for the role of king. Was that fair? Defend your answer.

**Behind the Scenes:** 1 Samuel 16:7

When 1 Samuel 16:7 tells us that "the LORD looks at the heart" it clearly does not mean that God judges us by the blood-pumping organ in our chests. But what exactly *does* it mean?

In this scriptural context, the word "heart" encompasses all the important, intangible things that make us who we really are. The heart is the core of someone's personality, values, and thinking. As such, it includes a person's moral and spiritual priorities, as well as that person's emotions, will, inward motivations, and thoughts.[12]

6. First Samuel 16:7 reveals that "the LORD looks at the heart." Why is that a big deal?

7. What if everyone could "look at the heart"? Do you think that would change any of your friendships or the way you and your friends treat other people?

8. If we'd met Samuel on the road right after his experience with David, what do you think he would've told us about God?

OPEN LIFE

9. What do you think God is looking for when he looks at your heart?

10. What will you do this week to help God find that?

**Parent Tip**

Encourage family members to be specific in the way they answer "Open Life" questions. Also, allow kids to wait a minute or two in silence before answering. This will give them an opportunity to think through their responses a bit before having to talk about them.

# 11

# The Bigger They Are . . .

The battle is the LORD's.
1 Samuel 17:47

THEME: **Courage**
SCRIPTURE: **1 Samuel 17:20–50**

## OPEN UP

1. Lots of things scare people, like thunder, spiders, heights, a new school, or even broccoli. What's your greatest fear? Why?

2. When have you seen a scary bully? What did you do?

**Parent Tip:** For Extra Fun

At the end of this discussion time, pass out 3 x 5 cards and color markers. Have everyone write "'The battle is the Lord's!'—1 Samuel 17:47" on their cards, and personalize their cards with drawings or designs as well. Encourage family members to keep their cards with them during the coming week as constant reminders to look to God for courage.

## OPEN BOOK

***Have family members read 1 Samuel 17:20–50.***

3. Goliath was definitely a scary bully. And David's brothers also bullied David a little bit. In what ways did God give David courage to face those people?

4. Like David, the Israelite warriors followed God—but they were afraid to face Goliath while David wasn't. Why was David different?

5. Without using the words *brave*, *guts*, or *fearless*, how would you describe David's courage?

**Behind the Scenes:** 1 Samuel 17:20–50

Goliath was a big guy—so much so that he's become history's unofficial definition of a giant. But what does that mean in today's terms? Consider this:

- With his armor on, Goliath probably stood close to ten feet tall—meaning the top of his head would've likely brushed up against the rim of a basketball hoop.
- The tip of his spear weighed around twenty pounds—about the same as one tire on your family car.
- His chest armor alone weighed about one hundred and fifty pounds—about as much as an average teenage boy weighs today.[13]

6. David acted with great courage when he faced Goliath. Do you think he was afraid and fought anyway, or do you think he wasn't afraid at all? Defend your answer.

7. When we feel afraid, how does God give us courage? What does that look like?

8. Acting with courage doesn't always guarantee victory. How can a person show courage in defeat?

## OPEN LIFE

9. When have you seen someone in our family act with courage? How did it make you feel? Describe it.

10. If David were here right now, what advice about courage would he give to help us during the coming week?

**Parent Tip**

Encourage family members to be specific in the way they answer "Open Life" questions. Also, allow kids to wait a minute or two in silence before answering. This will give them an opportunity to think through their responses a bit before having to talk about them.

# 12

# Bountiful Bread Crumbs

I have directed a widow there to supply you with food.
1 Kings 17:9

THEME: **God's Faithfulness/Thanksgiving**
SCRIPTURE: **1 Kings 17:7–16**

## OPEN UP

1. When I count to three, hold your breath for as long as you can. Ready? One, two, three! While you're not breathing, think about this: What if God stopped providing oxygen for us each day? What would we do?

2. We depend on God every day for things like oxygen and keeping the sun in our sky—yet we often don't even notice his constant faithfulness toward us. What other things does God do that we seem to take for granted?

**OPEN BOOK**

***Have family members read 1 Kings 17:7–16.***

3. What are your first impressions of Elijah and the widow in this story? Explain.

4. How did God show his faithfulness to Elijah? How did God show his faithfulness to the widow?

5. God could have easily turned the widow's supplies into a great feast without Elijah being there, and he could have easily provided plenty of food for Elijah without the help of the widow. Why didn't he do either of those things?

**Behind the Scenes:** 1 Kings 17:9, 12

It's interesting to discover that the widow of Zarephath was (a) not an Israelite (she was actually Phoenician), and (b) not someone who followed the Hebrew God. Some commentators have even suggested she was "heathen"—that is, a pagan who had rejected Elijah's God entirely up to this point in her life (see 1 Kings 17:12).[14]

In spite of that, God both chose and used her to accomplish his purpose. "I have directed a widow there to supply you with food," he told Elijah (1 Kings 17:9). This widow appeared to have no idea that God was directing her, yet she obeyed anyway—and God rewarded that faith with provision for each day. This seems to be more proof that our God can use anyone—even those who deny him—to fulfill his promises and accomplish his purpose in our lives.

6. Do you think God is obligated to make your life easy? Defend your answer.

7. The widow didn't seem to know that God had chosen to use her. Do you think God ever uses you without you knowing it? Explain how that might work.

8. How do you know when God wants to use you to show his faithfulness to others? What do you do about it?

## OPEN LIFE

9. If you could wake up tomorrow and see everything God does for you all day long, how do you think that would impact the way you lived out your day?

10. What are three things we can do this week to help us be more thankful for God's faithfulness toward us each day?

**Parent Tip:** For Extra Fun

At the end of this devotion, pull out some craft supplies and have each person in your family make a personalized "Thank You" card for God. Hang the cards on your refrigerator for a week as a reminder of Christ's constant faithfulness to your family.

**Parent Tip**

Encourage family members to be specific in the way they answer "Open Life" questions. Also, allow kids to wait a minute or two in silence before answering. This will give them an opportunity to think through their responses a bit before having to talk about them.

# 13

# The Lord Is . . .

I will fear no evil, for you are with me.
Psalm 23:4

THEME: **God's Presence**
SCRIPTURE: **Psalm 23**

## OPEN UP

1. Imagine you could create the safest, most peaceful place on earth. What would this place be like? Describe it.
2. Tell about a time you felt completely cared for and loved. What do you remember about it?

**Parent Tip:** For Extra Fun

If your kids are the creative writing type, they might have fun doing this "personalization" writing exercise. Give everyone paper and pencils, and challenge kids to rewrite every verse of Psalm 23 as if it were a letter from King David to each child.

OPEN BOOK

***Have family members read Psalm 23.***

3. According to Psalm 23, being near God made King David (the author) feel safe and loved. Why do you think he felt that way?

4. God is our shepherd who keeps us safe and cared for, but how does that happen exactly? Explain it as best you can.

5. We know that King David often endured very unpleasant times in his life, and he had many enemies who hurt him. So how could he say the things he did in Psalm 23? Was he just faking it? Defend your answer.

**Behind the Scenes:** Psalm 23:1

There are few images of God in Scripture more evocative than that described in Psalm 23:1, "The Lord is my shepherd." This word picture is filled with intimacy and authority for us as God's figurative sheep. "The biblical imagery [of God as our Shepherd] stresses the care and compassion of the divine shepherd," Bible scholars tell us, "and the dependence of people on God to meet all their needs."

As such, Psalm 23 and other biblical references use this shepherd image to show God as our safe guide for life, as our protector, savior, gatherer, and provider. Additionally, our good Shepherd is presented as having tender love for the weakest of his sheep, as carrying and caring for us when we're hurt or lost, as the central figure around whom our lives revolve, and—perhaps most importantly—as the selfless, sacrificial leader willing to die that we might live.[15]

6. What kinds of unpleasant times do we experience today? (For instance, at school, on a trip, at home, or when playing sports.)

7. How might knowing that God is near help you when you're feeling discouraged or unhappy during those unpleasant times?

8. David said that God guides us in the "paths of righteousness." How would you explain that to your best friend?

## OPEN LIFE

9. If you had to summarize all of Psalm 23 in only one sentence, what would you say?

10. What will you do to help yourself remember that sentence for the rest of this week?

**Parent Tip**

Encourage family members to be specific in the way they answer "Open Life" questions. Also, allow kids to wait a minute or two in silence before answering. This will give them an opportunity to think through their responses a bit before having to talk about them.

# 14

# Noisy Is Good!

Let everything that has breath praise the LORD.
Psalm 150:6

THEME: **Worship**
SCRIPTURE: **Psalm 150**

## OPEN UP

1. If you could not use words to worship God, what would you do? Show me.

2. What do you think it means to praise the Lord? Let's create a new definition for the dictionary.

**Parent Tip:** For Extra Fun

After this devotion, take your kids to a local musical instrument store. Let kids browse a bit, and ask them to demonstrate (carefully) how they might use today's instruments to follow the instructions of Psalm 150.

OPEN BOOK

***Have family members read Psalm 150.***

3. For this psalmist, what does it mean to praise the Lord? Explain it as if you were talking to someone who had never heard of God before.

4. The worship experience described in Psalm 150 would be awfully noisy—in fact, it sounds more like a party than a church service. What do you think about that?

5. Who gets more out of worship: God or us? Defend your answer.

**Behind the Scenes:** Psalm 150:1–2, 6

The phrase translated "praise the LORD" in Psalm 150:1 and 150:6 is actually a single Hebrew word: *halleluyah*, which we've transliterated today as "hallelujah." It derives from a combination of the words *halal* ("praise") and *Yah* ("God").

What's important here is that the psalmist is not simply suggesting, or even strongly recommending, that everything with breath *halleluyah*. The grammatical construction here is in the imperative, issued as a command. Why? Because God's "acts of power" and "surpassing greatness" (v. 2) fairly demand such a joyous, zealous response from his people! To do anything less would simply not be enough.[16]

6. Psalm 150:2 tells us to worship God for his greatness. In your opinion, what makes God so great? Include examples from your own life.

7. According to Psalm 150, music can play an important part in worship. Why do you suppose that's true?

8. Music can also lead people away from worshiping God. Why does that happen?

## OPEN LIFE

9. The psalmist never indicates that worship should happen only on Sunday. How might we worship God on a Monday at school? Or on a Saturday? Let's brainstorm ideas for every day of the week.

10. Which of these ideas will you try out this week?

**Parent Tip**

Encourage family members to be specific in the way they answer "Open Life" questions. Also, allow kids to wait a minute or two in silence before answering. This will give them an opportunity to think through their responses a bit before having to talk about them.

# 15

# Smart Sayings

> Do not be wise in your own eyes.
>
> Proverbs 3:7

THEME: **Wisdom**
SCRIPTURE: **Proverbs 3:3–8**

## OPEN UP

1. The Awesome Publishing House called! They want us to write a book called *Awesome Advice for Families*. What wise words will we include in our book?

2. How can you tell if something is good advice? Let's make a list of qualifications to help us recognize it.

**Parent Tip:** For Extra Fun

If you have the time and the interest, go ahead and have your family write a little "book" of awesome advice for families. Collect everyone's ideas into a computer file, and then print it all with a cover page. Let kids decorate the cover with their own designs, and give each person in your family his or her own copy.

## OPEN BOOK

***Have family members read Proverbs 3:3–8.***

3. Which of our qualifications for good advice do you see displayed in the wisdom from Proverbs 3? Explain.

4. What do you think it means to "bind" love and faithfulness to you? How do people like you and me do that?

5. What does it look like when someone trusts in the Lord with all of his or her heart? If you can, give examples of people you know.

**Behind the Scenes:** Proverbs 3:3

The encouragement of Proverbs 3:3 for us to "bind" love and faithfulness around our necks may have been inspired by the common use of phylacteries in ancient Israel. A phylactery is a small leather box containing key quotes from Scripture. Jewish people often tied it to their hand or strapped it to their forehead as a reminder of God's law and love.[17]

In spite of that literal, physical inspiration, the context of this passage indicates a more figurative representation of truth: in the same way a beautiful necklace enhances the wearer's attractiveness, a lifestyle adorned by love and faithfulness adds special, eternal beauty to a person.

6. If you were to draw a picture of someone who is "wise in his own eyes," what would you draw? Why?

7. How does a person avoid being "wise in his (or her) own eyes"? Give ideas.

8. If you were to summarize Proverbs 3:3–8 in one sentence or one wise saying that you could share with your friends, what would it be? Take a moment to think about it.

## OPEN LIFE

9. What's one thing you discovered from Proverbs 3:3–8 and from our discussion today that you'd like to remember a year from now?

10. This week, how can we help each other remember God's awesome advice in Proverbs 3:3–8?

**Parent Tip**

Encourage family members to be specific in the way they answer "Open Life" questions. Also, allow kids to wait a minute or two in silence before answering. This will give them an opportunity to think through their responses a bit before having to talk about them.

# 16

# Parent Power

My son, keep your father's command.
Proverbs 6:20

THEME: **Parents/Mother's Day or Father's Day**
SCRIPTURE: **Proverbs 6:20–23**

## OPEN UP

1. What if all parents in the world went on vacation to Mars for a month and left their kids to fend for themselves? What would you like about that? What would you dislike?
2. Why do you think God gave you parents? Explain.

**Parent Tip:** For Extra Fun

This devotion works well the night before either Mother's Day or Father's Day. Follow it up with a celebration of family in anticipation of the parent holiday to come. For instance, you might share cake, play games, or pop popcorn and watch a movie—anything that's fun for all and allows you to hang out together for a while.

## OPEN BOOK

***Have family members read Proverbs 6:20–23.***

3. What do you see as a parent's responsibilities in this Scripture? What do you see as a child's responsibilities?

4. Why do you think the Bible describes a parent's leadership as a lamp and a light (see Prov. 6:23)? What does that mean, really?

5. What happens when a parent or a child doesn't live out Proverbs 6:20–23 at home? How does that affect their relationship? Their life outside home?

**Behind the Scenes:** Proverbs 6:20–23

During medieval times, older monks needed a way to teach their younger students ("novices") how to write. They came up with an insightful plan: novices in a monastery were often required to copy, over and over, the book of Proverbs. In this way, the students learned helpful writing skills and, at the same time, internalized wise teachings like those found in Proverbs 6:20–23.[18]

6. What do you think makes it hard for a parent to live out Proverbs 6:20–23 consistently every day? What makes it easier?

7. When do you feel like it's hard to listen to your parents and follow their leadership and discipline? When is it easy? Why?

8. How does God help us build healthy relationships like those described in this Scripture? Give examples.

## OPEN LIFE

9. No one is perfect—neither parents nor children. We all make mistakes that hurt one another sometimes. What's the best response when that happens in our family?

10. What can we do to help each other become better at living out the teaching of Proverbs 6:20–23 every day this week? Let's brainstorm ideas.

**Parent Tip**

Encourage family members to be specific in the way they answer "Open Life" questions. Also, allow kids to wait a minute or two in silence before answering. This will give them an opportunity to think through their responses a bit before having to talk about them.

# 17

# God's on the Clock

There is a time for everything.
Ecclesiastes 3:1

THEME: **God's Timing**
SCRIPTURE: **Ecclesiastes 3:1–13**

## OPEN UP

1. We've been challenged to enter the World's Greatest Watch contest! All we have to do now is design the world's greatest watch. What kinds of features should we include?

2. What would it be like if no one in the world had a watch or a clock to keep track of time?

**Parent Tip:** For Extra Fun

Grab a bucket of sidewalk chalk and find some open concrete. Decorate that empty space with a row of "designer" watches created by your family members. Be sure to draw a price tag next to each watch ($1 million anyone?).

OPEN BOOK

*Have family members read Ecclesiastes 3:1–13.*

3. What does this passage tell us about God's timekeeping?

4. If you were to design a watch based on Ecclesiastes 3:1–13, what kind of features would it have?

5. This Scripture indicates that God allows both good and bad things to happen in our lives. Why does God do that?

**Behind the Scenes:** Ecclesiastes

There is a question over who actually wrote Ecclesiastes. The author named in the book is *Koheleth* (translated as "teacher" or "preacher" in Eccles. 1:1, 1:12, and subsequently throughout the book). However, the author also writes as if from the perspective of King Solomon, the son of David. For some scholars, this is simply a literary device akin to Mark Twain writing from the perspective of Huckleberry Finn. For others, this indicates (along with other clues) that Solomon was the actual author and that he used *Koheleth* as a pen name of sorts (much the same way Samuel Clemens used the pen name Mark Twain).[19]

Regardless of who the actual author was, Ecclesiastes uses the life and experiences of King Solomon as the backdrop to deliver the message that true joy in life is a generous gift from God alone (see Eccles. 2:24–25; 3:13). As one commentator points out, "One of the words used most frequently in Ecclesiastes to describe God's relationship to individuals is the verb 'to give.' It appears eleven times with God as the subject."[20]

6. How does it make you feel to know that God has created a time for everything—both good and bad—in your own life? Try to use colors to describe your feelings. For example,

"Blue, because I feel worried about it sometimes," or "Red, because it's kind of exciting."

7. Ecclesiastes 3:11 says, "He has made everything beautiful in its time." What does that mean? Explain it as if you were talking to a space alien visiting Earth for the first time.

8. If you could ask God one question about Ecclesiastes 3:1–13, what would you ask? How do you think he'd answer?

## OPEN LIFE

9. When bad things happen, it's often tempting to think that God isn't paying attention. How might Ecclesiastes 3:1–13 help us when we feel like that?

10. Ecclesiastes 3:8 tells us that God has made "a time to love." With Jesus, we can experience that "time" every day. How can we also share it with others this week?

**Parent Tip**

Encourage family members to be specific in the way they answer "Open Life" questions. Also, allow kids to wait a minute or two in silence before answering. This will give them an opportunity to think through their responses a bit before having to talk about them.

# 18

# Dem Bones, Dem Bones

They say, "Our bones are dried up and our hope is gone."
Ezekiel 37:11

THEME: **Hope**
SCRIPTURE: **Ezekiel 37:1–14**

## OPEN UP

1. What's the most unusual thing you've ever seen with your own eyes? Describe it.
2. God often works in unusual ways. When do you think that's happened with you? Tell about a time you remember.

**Parent Tip:** For Extra Fun

Take a digital camera and have everyone in your family go for a walk around your neighborhood. Have family members take turns pointing out anything unusual that they see while you walk, and take a quick picture of it. Later, view your pics on a computer and vote to decide which was the most unusual thing of all.

OPEN BOOK

***Have family members read Ezekiel 37:1–14.***

3. If Ezekiel were here today, he'd probably say that the most unusual thing he ever saw was when God brought to life an entire army before his very eyes! What do you think Ezekiel felt while that was happening? What would you have felt?

4. At the time, Ezekiel was very sad because his country had been overpowered, scattered, and enslaved by its enemies. When you feel sad, what do you do?

5. It was easy for God to raise up an army from dry, dead bones. How does it make you feel to know that he has that kind of power?

**Behind the Scenes:** Ezekiel 37:1–14

The prophet Ezekiel lived during the same time as Daniel and Jeremiah. We would call him a "preacher's kid"—that is, he grew up in a family of priests living in Judah. When he was twenty-five years old (in 597 BC), King Nebuchadnezzar conquered Jerusalem, and his troops carried off Ezekiel and his wife into captivity. They were forced to resettle near Babylon in a town called Tel-abib. Five years later, Ezekiel began to speak as a prophet of God. At first he spoke primarily of God's coming judgment on the nation of Judah. After that happened, his prophecies changed and became messages of hope and restoration for God's people.[21]

Ezekiel's book is known for its unique symbolic imagery and the "presentation of future events, both political and spiritual, in a 'hidden' way; that is, a way that is not immediately clear in its interpretation." Additionally, scholars have long argued over whether the events described in Ezekiel are literal (actual events) or figurative (symbolic or visionary, but not actual events). As such, the "valley of dry bones" experience in Ezekiel 37 may have actually happened, or as most believe, it may have been a symbolic vision that only Ezekiel saw.[22]

6. Finish this sentence: "Knowing that God is all-powerful, and that he loves me, makes me feel . . ."

7. Just as God allowed Ezekiel to experience hard times, sometimes he allows bad things to happen in our lives. Since God's so powerful, why doesn't he just make our lives easy and trouble-free?

8. After this vision, Ezekiel's circumstances hadn't changed—but he had changed. How do you think Ezekiel felt after he watched God raise up this army?

## OPEN LIFE

9. If Ezekiel were here right now, what do you think he'd want to tell us?

10. How can God help us to trust and hope in him when we feel sad this week?

### Parent Tip

Encourage family members to be specific in the way they answer "Open Life" questions. Also, allow kids to wait a minute or two in silence before answering. This will give them an opportunity to think through their responses a bit before having to talk about them.

# 19

# A God Risk

> Daniel resolved not to defile himself with the royal food and wine.
>
> Daniel 1:8

THEME: **Purity/Obedience**
SCRIPTURE: **Daniel 1:1–20**

## OPEN UP

1. What's the meaning of your name? Does the meaning fit you?
2. What if you could officially change your name? What would you pick for a new one?

**Parent Tip:** For Extra Fun

When answering questions 1 and 2, gather everyone around a computer and visit a website like babynames.com or thinkbabynames.com. That should help you add a few interesting ideas to the mix!

OPEN BOOK

***Have family members read Daniel 1:1–20.***

3. When Daniel was taken as a slave, his masters changed his name to Belteshazzar—a name that actually honored a pagan god. How did Daniel's actions show his commitment to the one true God, despite his new name?

4. It was hard to stay obedient to God and not get punished by his new masters, but Daniel managed to pull it off. How do you think he did it? (Let's act it out as if we were there!)

5. Daniel decided ahead of time what was important. He knew what he would and wouldn't do as a servant of God. Why was that important?

**Behind the Scenes:** Daniel 1:6–7

The Babylonian name given to Daniel, "Belteshazzar," was actually a shortened version of a prayer for protection from the pagan god Bel. Additionally, when spoken, the god Marduk was often attached to the beginning of the name, as in Marduk-Belteshazzar.[23]

It's interesting to note that even though Daniel's captors tried to brand him with the name of a false god, the truth won out. In the end, despite the demands of his Babylonian name, Daniel has been known for countless generations as a faithful follower of the one true God, while Bel and Marduk have largely been forgotten.

6. Do you think it made a difference that Daniel and his friends acted together in obedience to God? Why or why not?

7. How do our friends help us to be obedient to God today? How do they sometimes lead us to be disobedient?

8. God honored Daniel and his friends for their obedience and determination to remain pure. In what ways does God honor people who do the same things today?

## OPEN LIFE

9. What can we learn from Daniel's example to help us be obedient followers of God today, no matter what happens?

10. What would you like to say to God about our discussion today? Let's pray that to him now.

**Parent Tip**

Encourage family members to be specific in the way they answer "Open Life" questions. Also, allow kids to wait a minute or two in silence before answering. This will give them an opportunity to think through their responses a bit before having to talk about them.

# 20

# Death before Dishonor

We will not serve your gods or worship the image of gold you have set up.

Daniel 3:18

THEME: **Risky Faith**
SCRIPTURE: **Daniel 3:1–28**

## OPEN UP

1. Hurricane, tornado, or earthquake: If you had to experience one of these right now, which would you choose?
2. When disasters like these hit, the true nature of people shows plainly in the way they respond. What are some examples of how that works? Describe them.

**Parent Tip:** For Extra Fun

If your kids are the dramatic type, it can be fun to act out this theatrical story in your living room. Choose one person to be the narrator (who reads the Scripture), and assign roles to the rest of the family so they can act out the events as the narrator reads them.

## OPEN BOOK

***Have family members read Daniel 3:1–28.***

3. Disaster hit Shadrach, Meshach, and Abednego when King Nebuchadnezzar demanded that they worship his statue. How did their response in that situation reveal their true nature?

4. What did this situation reveal about King Nebuchadnezzar?

5. These three men knew God *could* save them, but it wasn't guaranteed that God *would* save them (see Dan. 3:17–18). Why were they willing to risk it?

**Behind the Scenes:** Daniel 3:1

The "image of gold" that King Nebuchadnezzar had constructed must have been impressive. By today's building standards, it would have risen about nine stories high! Yet at only nine feet wide, it would also have been remarkably narrow for such a tall structure. Add gold plating and human features (representing Babylonian gods) to the spire-like sculpture, and it would have been hard for anyone to ignore.[24]

6. What makes it risky to serve God wholeheartedly today?

7. What happens when we are *not* willing to risk following God?

8. Imagine that Shadrach, Meshach, and Abednego are coming to speak at our church. What will they tell us about risky faith?

## OPEN LIFE

9. How can we know when we must take a risk for God and when risk is not really required? Let's make a list of guidelines.

10. If you had the courage to risk standing up for your faith every day this week, how might that change things?

**Parent Tip**

Encourage family members to be specific in the way they answer "Open Life" questions. Also, allow kids to wait a minute or two in silence before answering. This will give them an opportunity to think through their responses a bit before having to talk about them.

# 21

# Stop. Start Again.

When God saw . . . how they turned from their evil ways, he relented and did not bring on them the destruction he had threatened.

Jonah 3:10

THEME: **Change of Heart/Repentance/ New Year's Day**
SCRIPTURE: **Jonah 3:1–10**

## OPEN UP

1. Our family has won an all-expenses-paid trip to anywhere on earth! Where will we choose to go?
2. Now, how will we get to our destination? We can choose from these modes of travel: hot air balloon, submarine, train, helicopter, or minivan.

**Parent Tip:** For Extra Fun

Pull out a map of Iraq, or look one up on the internet. Find the modern city of Mosul and show it to your kids. If possible, include pictures of the people and the lifestyle there. Tell your family members this is where the city of Nineveh was originally located, though now it has been lost and buried under Mosul. Use the map and your pictures as a backdrop for your discussion time with Jonah 3.

## OPEN BOOK

***Have family members read Jonah 3:1–10.***

3. Jonah didn't have a choice as to whether or not he would preach God's message in Nineveh, but the people of Nineveh had a choice about how they would respond. What impresses you about their reaction?

4 The king commanded that even the animals be covered with sackcloth, a type of clothing that people wore for funerals. What's the deal with that?

5. What do you think it meant for the Ninevites to "turn from their evil ways"? What choices were involved?

**Behind the Scenes:** Jonah 3:1–10

At the time of Jonah, Nineveh was a thriving city in the empire of Assyria, ideally located at the junction of the Tigris and Khosr rivers. Archaeologists excavating Nineveh in modern times have discovered remains of an advanced society that featured "public squares, parks, botanical gardens, and even a zoo." Today, the site of ancient Nineveh sits under the modern city of Mosul, Iraq.[25]

When Jonah preached his message of doom to the ancient Ninevites, the people there immediately repented. In that time, fasting and wearing sackcloth were "demonstrations of mourning" that indicated their intense sorrow at God's coming judgment.[26] God honored their actions and spared their city.

> Centuries later, Jesus pointed to the people of Nineveh as a shining example of the appropriate way to respond to God's Word (see Matt. 12:41).

6. What does it mean for people like you and me to "turn from our evil ways"?

7. Imagine we're reporters for the Nineveh daily newspaper. We've been assigned to write an article titled "Change of Heart Changes Entire City!" What will we say in that article?

8. The people of Nineveh had a radical change of heart, turning away from selfishness and toward God. What do you think would happen if the same thing took place here in our home, or in your school?

9. The king of Nineveh led his people in their turn back toward God. Who are leaders in our lives that can help lead us back to God when we need it? How do they help us?

## OPEN LIFE

10. Everybody falls short, and sometimes we turn away from God. What can we do when we realize we need a change of heart so we can turn back toward God?

11. In what ways can we encourage our friends and family to seek God this week? Let's brainstorm ideas!

> **Parent Tip**
>
> Encourage family members to be specific in the way they answer "Open Life" questions. Also, allow kids to wait a minute or two in silence before answering. This will give them an opportunity to think through their responses a bit before having to talk about them.

# 22

# Just What Does God Want from Me?

He has showed you, O mortal, what is good.
Micah 6:8

THEME: **Faithful Living**
SCRIPTURE: **Micah 6:6–8**

## OPEN UP

1. The Rules Committee called! They want us to come up with the top three rules people should follow for a *really* good day. What should we tell them?

2. What kinds of unspoken rules do we follow in a normal day? How are they similar to or different from our top three rules for a really good day?

**Parent Tip:** For Extra Fun

Why not go ahead and write an all-new song that uses Micah 6:6–8 as the source for the lyrics? Invite the whole family to get creative and sing along!

OPEN BOOK

3. If the Rules Committee called God looking for ideas about three rules for a really good day, what do you think God would say? Why?

4. In what ways would following God's rules make for a good day? For a good life?

*Have family members read Micah 6:6–8*

5. What do you hear this Scripture saying to us?

**Behind the Scenes:** Micah 6:8

At the time Micah wrote his book, many Israelites viewed the ritual of animal sacrifice as a sort of "get out of jail free card." It was common, for instance, for a wealthy person to exploit, abuse, or even steal from a poorer family. Instead of making amends for that crime—and vowing to avoid that kind of sin in the future—the abuser would simply offer a sin sacrifice at the temple and assume that settled the matter as far as God was concerned.[27]

Through Micah, though, God made it clear that right relationships with others (to do justly and love mercy) and with God (to walk humbly) are what really matter in life. Without them, everything else is just meaningless, empty ritual.

6. At the time this was written, people tried to impress God with all kinds of animal sacrifices and burnt offerings. What do people do today to try to impress God? Why isn't God impressed?

7. What do you think it means to act justly? To love mercy? To walk humbly with God?

8. God's top three rules, according to Micah 6:8, are all about how we live out friendship with him and with others. Why do you think that's so important to God?

## OPEN LIFE

9. If someone asked you to write a song about what Micah 6:6–8 means, using your own lyrics, what would you say? (If you're gutsy, go ahead and sing your answer!)

10. What if we couldn't use words to explain this Scripture? How might our attitude and actions during the coming week show people God's top three rules at work in our lives? Give examples.

**Parent Tip**

Encourage family members to be specific in the way they answer "Open Life" questions. Also, instruct kids to wait a minute or two in silence before answering. This will give them an opportunity to think through their responses a bit before having to talk about them.

# 23

# Help!

The LORD is good.
Nahum 1:7

THEME: **God's Protective Care**
SCRIPTURE: **Nahum 1:7**

## OPEN UP

1. If you were to design a brand-new superhero suit, what secret weapons would you include in it?

2. How would you use that super suit? Describe the situations and what you'd do.

**Parent Tip:** For Extra Fun

During the week after this devotion, send a note in your child's lunch or backpack each day that creatively reminds him or her of Nahum 1:7. You might write the verse in your own words, draw a picture illustrating something from your discussion, or just send a cheery "Remember Nahum 1:7 today!" encouragement.

## OPEN BOOK

***Have family members read Nahum 1:7.***

3. According to this verse, God is like a secret weapon in our lives. How do you think that works?

4. Nahum 1:7 tells us that the Lord is good, but if God is good then why do bad things sometimes happen to us? Explain.

5. If bad things happen, does that mean God is not keeping the promise made in Nahum 1:7? Defend your answer.

**Behind the Scenes:** Nahum 1:7

When Jonah preached repentance to Nineveh (the capital city of the Assyrian Empire) the people there turned to God and were spared. About a hundred years later, the Assyrians had once again turned away from God. Enter the prophet Nahum, who pronounced God's coming judgment upon the Assyrian Empire and on Nineveh. This military devastation occurred in 612 BC, a destruction so complete that the city was never rebuilt. It was eventually covered, literally, by the sands of time.[28]

In the midst of this violent upheaval, thousands of Israelites were living in Nineveh under the oppressive hand of their Assyrian captors. Nahum spoke hope directly to these people, promising that God would be their refuge (Nahum 1:7). The Hebrew word translated *refuge* here (or *stronghold* in some versions) refers to a heavily fortified place. It suggests the picture of a fortress made of impenetrable rock.[29] In other words, in even the worst circumstances God's protection for his followers is secure and trustworthy—regardless of what happens.

6. Nahum wrote this message to people who were living under threat of war. What do you think it meant to them when Nahum promised God would be their refuge?

7. What do you think it means for God to be our refuge today? Explain.

8. Nahum 1:7 insists that God cares for those who trust in him. How do we know that's true?

## OPEN LIFE

9. God's protective care for us is always part of our lives—but not always what we expect it to be. How can Nahum 1:7 help us to trust God even when our lives are going differently than we expected?

10. What's one thing we can do this week to remind each other that God is good, that he is our refuge, and that he cares for us? Let's brainstorm ideas.

**Parent Tip**

Encourage family members to be specific in the way they answer "Open Life" questions. Also, allow kids to wait a minute or two in silence before answering. This will give them an opportunity to think through their responses a bit before having to talk about them.

# 24

# Are You There, God?

How long, LORD, must I call for help?
Habakkuk 1:2

THEME: **Unanswered Prayer**
SCRIPTURE: **Habakkuk 1:2–5**

## OPEN UP

1. "Mom? Mom? Mom? Mom?" How does it feel when someone doesn't answer you?
2. What if God stopped listening to our prayers? What would we do?

**Parent Tip:** For Extra Fun

Have family members each tell about a time when they felt absolutely certain God answered one of their prayers. Then write those stories in a letter to each child. Seal each letter and on the front of the envelope write, "When God seems silent, open this!" Give the letters to your kids to keep nearby for future use.

**OPEN BOOK**

***Have family members read Habakkuk 1:2–5.***

3. Re-read these verses, and try to place yourself in Habakkuk's shoes. What were people like Habakkuk feeling when God didn't answer them?

4. We know that God really is listening to us at all times. So why does God allow us to go through times when it feels like he's not listening?

5. What do you think it means when God doesn't answer our prayers right away, or in the way we expected him to answer?

**Behind the Scenes:** Habakkuk

It was sometime between 610 and 605 BC when the book of Habakkuk was written. The brutal Assyrian Empire ruled Judah through a puppet king, Jehoiakim. By today's standards, King Jehoiakim might be compared to a despot like Iraq's Saddam Hussein or Libya's Moammar Gadhafi. Under his rule, people murdered their children as sacrifices to pagan deities, and prophets of the true God were oppressed, arrested, and even killed.

Into these horrible circumstances Habakkuk appeared. Unlike those of his contemporaries Ezekiel and Jeremiah, Habakkuk's prophecies were primarily complaints to God—asking out loud why God allows evil to flourish in our world. This makes the book of Habakkuk unique. As one commentator put it, "Most prophets speak to the people on God's behalf. Habakkuk . . . spoke to God on behalf of the people."[30]

6. Does silence mean God doesn't care about us? Explain.

7. Which is more likely: God is not listening to us, or we are not listening to God? Defend your answer.

8. When God seems silent, how can we continue to trust him? Let's brainstorm a list of ideas.

## OPEN LIFE

9. In the end, God promises that we will be "utterly amazed" by what he does for us. In what ways has God been amazing in our lives so far?

10. What would you like to say to God right now? Let's pray that as our closing.

**Parent Tip**

Encourage family members to be specific in the way they answer "Open Life" questions. Also, allow kids to wait a minute or two in silence before answering. This will give them an opportunity to think through their responses a bit before having to talk about them.

# 25

# Be Strong—God Is Stronger

Be strong. . . . For I am with you.
Haggai 2:4

THEME: **Discouragement**
SCRIPTURE: **Haggai 2:1–9**

## OPEN UP

1. When someone you care about is feeling discouraged, what do you say to them? Why?

2. During the time the prophet Haggai lived, the temple of God had been destroyed and left in ruins by invading armies. The people of Israel felt discouraged and hopeless. If you had been there, what would you have said to encourage them?

**Parent Tip:** For Extra Fun

Have kids create a few "encouragement" cards that summarize or illustrate messages from Haggai 2:1–9. Keep them on hand to share with friends or family members who are going through a discouraging time.

OPEN BOOK

***Have family members read Haggai 2:1–9.***

3. How did God try to encourage the people of Israel through Haggai?

4. Verse 4 tells God's followers to be strong because God is with us. Why is that encouraging for us?

5. In Haggai 2:5, God tells his people not to be afraid. Why do you think he said that?

**Behind the Scenes:** Haggai

The prophet Haggai is very much a mystery man. Theologian Clyde Francisco reports, "Haggai appears suddenly in 520 BC, and disappears as suddenly. Nothing is known of his life before or after his preaching." Francisco suggests that Haggai was an old man at the time of his prophecy—which was important because it would mean that he had been alive to see God's temple in Jerusalem before it was destroyed by invading armies.

At this time in history, the glory of that temple was nothing but a vanished memory. The Jews had been banished into captivity, first by Assyrian armies and then by Babylonian forces. Upon returning at last to Jerusalem they were greeted by ruins, poverty, religious indifference, and hostile neighbors. It would take courage to rebuild God's temple in this environment of utter defeat—so God sent Haggai to give his people supernatural encouragement to overcome.[31]

6. God promised to rebuild the temple as a sign of his glory and presence with his people. Today, each of us is a personal temple for God. How do we see his glory and presence in our lives?

7. Verse 8 declares that God has plenty to provide whatever is needed, even enough to build an enormous temple. How does that make you feel? Explain.

8. If Haggai had been with you the last time you felt discouraged, what do you think he would've said to you? How would that have made a difference?

## OPEN LIFE

9. Everyone feels discouraged sometimes, but no one has to be alone when feeling discouraged. How can we take advantage of the fact that God is with us the next time we feel discouraged?

10. What's one thing you'd like to say to God about Haggai 2:1–9? Let's tell him that right now.

**Parent Tip**

Encourage family members to be specific in the way they answer "Open Life" questions. Also, allow kids to wait a minute or two in silence before answering. This will give them an opportunity to think through their responses a bit before having to talk about them.

# 26

# Kindness Counts

Show mercy and compassion to one another.
Zechariah 7:9

THEME: **Compassion/National Compassion Holiday**
SCRIPTURE: **Zechariah 7:8–12**

## OPEN UP

1. It's time for the Kindness and Compassion Awards—and we're all winners! As part of our awards ceremony, answer this question: What's one way the person on your right has been kind to you in the past? Tell about it.

2. How do you feel when someone acts kindly toward you? Explain.

**Parent Tip:** For Extra Fun

Although not yet official, National Compassion Holiday falls on March 15 each year. This holiday is meant to encourage volunteer service to aid senior centers and disabled-care facilities. If you and your family experience this devotion near that date, consider finding a way to help out in the spirit of this holiday! Learn more at www.nationalcompassionholiday.com.

## OPEN BOOK

***Have family members read Zechariah 7:8–12.***

3. Why do you think God cares whether or not we're kind to each other?
4. What happens in our friendships when people are kind and compassionate to each other?
5. What happens in our home when family members are unkind to each other?

**Behind the Scenes:** Zechariah 7:8–9

The prophet/priest Zechariah was born a captive in Babylonia. He was one of the Jewish exiles who returned to Jerusalem in 538 BC. A younger contemporary of Haggai, he worked with him to bring about the rebuilding of God's temple. Still, Zechariah is best known for his prophecies concerning the coming Messiah. For instance, it was Zechariah who famously, and accurately, predicted that the Messiah would come into Jerusalem riding on a donkey (see Zech. 9:9 and Matt. 21:1–5).[32]

Although Zechariah 7:8–9 is not considered a messianic prophesy, its fervent call for a lifestyle of compassion is a beautiful description of Jesus as well. When Christ walked this earth, this prophet's words were displayed in Jesus as living, breathing reality! And in Christ we have the ultimate example of compassion for us all to see, admire, and imitate.

6. In what ways do you think Jesus lived out the instructions of Zechariah 7:8–9? Tell a story about him.

7. If they told stories tomorrow about how you lived out Zechariah 7:8–9, what kinds of stories would you like people to tell?

8. How does Jesus help us to be kind and compassionate to one another every day?

## OPEN LIFE

9. If Jesus were a visitor in our home this week, what might we do to be kind and compassionate to him?

10. What might happen if we did those kind things for each other this week? Let's find out!

**Parent Tip**

Encourage family members to be specific in the way they answer "Open Life" questions. Also, allow kids to wait a minute or two in silence before answering. This will give them an opportunity to think through their responses a bit before having to talk about them.

SECTION 2

# Discussion Guides about the New Testament

# 27

# Bearing Gifts, We've Traveled Afar . . .

> We saw his star when it rose and have come to worship him.
>
> Matthew 2:2

THEME: **Jesus's Birth/Christmas**
SCRIPTURE: **Matthew 2:1–12**

## OPEN UP

1. What if you could go back in time and visit—for sixty seconds only—the wise men who gave gifts to baby Jesus? Would you want to visit them before or after they met Jesus? Why?
2. What advice would you give those wise men when you met them? Explain.

**Parent Tip:** For Extra Fun

If your children enjoy shopping, and if it is indeed the Christmas season, take everyone to a nearby mall for this devotion. Get some snacks and head to a table in the food court, surrounded by Christmas decorations and holiday music on the loudspeakers. Going through this devotion in that atmosphere will add a unique perspective to your discussion together.

## OPEN BOOK

3. The story of the wise men happened more than two thousand years ago, but it's still a popular part of Christmas celebrations. What do you think people like so much about this story?

***Have family members read Matthew 2:1–12.***

4. What's your impression of the wise men, or Magi, after reading Matthew 2:1–12? What words would you use to describe them?

**Behind the Scenes:** Matthew 2:2

The identity of the star that pointed the Magi toward the baby Jesus has been a subject of much curiosity for thousands of years.

The wise men of old likely viewed it as a heavenly "fravashi"—that is, the angel of, or astronomical counterpart to, the Messiah. Others have noted that Jupiter and Saturn were in close conjunction around the time of Christ's birth, and have speculated those planets, close together, appeared as a single bright star. Also, astronomers believe that Halley's comet flew over the Middle East during a time that could have been concurrent with Jesus's birth—and speculate that perhaps that was described as this "star" in the historical record.[1]

> Regardless of what it was, or how it got there, the final fact is that wise men of antiquity did see *something* that resembled an unusually bright star—and it led them directly to Jesus.

5. Why do you think the wise men thought it was necessary to give gifts to the baby Jesus?

6. The Magi said they traveled all the way to Bethlehem in order to "worship" the baby. How did they do that when they saw him? And what part did gift-giving have in that worship?

7. These wise men were in a foreign land, being watched by angry, murderous King Herod. Why were they willing to risk making Herod angry at them by worshiping baby Jesus and giving him expensive gifts?

8. The wise men had no idea that they'd be remembered for thousands of years simply because they gave gifts to a baby. Do you think they'd have done anything differently if they'd known? Explain.

## OPEN LIFE

9. If you could be remembered for giving one special gift to Jesus, what would you want it to be? Why?

10. This week, what can you do each day that would be like giving a special gift to Jesus? Let's brainstorm ideas!

**Parent Tip**

Encourage family members to be specific in the way they answer "Open Life" questions. Also, instruct kids to wait a minute or two in silence before answering. This will give them an opportunity to think through their responses a bit before having to talk about them.

# 28

# Under Water

Suddenly a furious storm came upon the lake.
Matthew 8:24

THEME: **Fear/Halloween**
SCRIPTURE: **Matthew 8:23–27**

## OPEN UP

1. Which would be scarier to find in our hometown (or on Halloween): (1) a giant octopus that can eat a house, (2) a giant plate of spinach that kids have to walk through to get to school, or (3) a giant lumberjack that eats both spinach and houses? Defend your answer.

2. Which of these do you find the most frightening: (1) lightning, (2) thunder, or (3) pouring rain? Explain your answer.

**Parent Tip:** For Extra Fun

Pull the cushions off your couch and/or living room chairs and spread them out on the floor. Tell kids that each cushion is a boat, and your living room floor is the ocean. Then "float" around in your boats while discussing today's story of Jesus calming the storm.

## OPEN BOOK

***Have family members read Matthew 8:23–27.***

3. What do you think the disciples were scared of the most when the storm overtook their boat? Imagine you were there, and share your ideas.

4. This storm was apparently very dangerous, and the disciples were afraid for their lives. How could Jesus sleep through something like that?

5. Jesus had never calmed a storm before, yet the disciples immediately turned to him for help when they were afraid. What keeps us from immediately turning to Jesus when we feel afraid?

**Behind the Scenes:** Matthew 8:23–27

It's tempting to view Jesus's disciples as a little bit cowardly in light of their panicked response to a little storm on a lake . . . until you realize that their lives (and the life of the sleeping Jesus) actually *were* in grave danger. The Sea of Galilee (also called Lake Gennesaret) sits six hundred feet below sea level in a gorge that runs north and south. The cold, swirling winds that sweep into this basin are often responsible for creating deadly conditions on the water.[2] The "furious storm" described in Matthew 8:24 was so severe that the literal translation of the Greek term here could actually be rendered as "great earthquake," indicating a disturbance of tsunami-like proportions.[3]

In this context, it would seem absurd to plead with a sleeping man to save you—and that speaks to the disciples' credit. When unable to save themselves, they cried for help from Christ, thereby acknowledging what many still refuse to believe: Jesus is indeed God Almighty.

6. Do you think Jesus cares when we're afraid? Why or why not?

7. How does faith in Jesus help us overcome fear?

8. Jesus easily calmed the storm for the disciples, but he doesn't always solve our problems so quickly. Why do you think he sometimes lets us endure uncomfortable "storms" in life?

## OPEN LIFE

9. Jesus has power over everything, even massive thunderstorms. Why is that important for us to know?

10. What's one thing you discovered today that you think is worth sharing with a friend? Who will you tell?

**Parent Tip**

Encourage family members to be specific in the way they answer "Open Life" questions. Also, allow kids to wait a minute or two in silence before answering. This will give them an opportunity to think through their responses a bit before having to talk about them.

# 29

# Who Is Jesus, Anyway?

You are the Messiah, the Son of the living God.
Matthew 16:16

THEME: **Jesus Christ**
SCRIPTURE: **Matthew 16:13–17**

## OPEN UP

1. Imagine you were interviewed on *The Nightly News on Mars* television show, and the alien newscaster said, "We've just heard that someone named Jesus Christ lived on your planet. Who is he?" What would you say?

2. Do you think it's important for people to decide who Jesus is? Why or why not?

**Parent Tip:** For Extra Fun

If your kids are the dramatic type, you might have fun acting out your answers to question 1 as a skit or a role-playing exercise. Be sure to ham it up with a cool "Mars accent" when you play the alien newscaster!

OPEN BOOK

***Have family members read Matthew 16:13–17.***

3. Why do you suppose Jesus asked his disciples who people thought he was?

4. If Jesus were to ask that same question today at your school, what do you think people would say about him?

5. A lot of people have different opinions about Jesus. How do we know who's right?

**Behind the Scenes:** Matthew 16:16

The word translated as "Christ" in the New Testament is *christos*, which in turn is the Greek translation of the Hebrew word *meshiah*—from which we get the word "Messiah." Its literal meaning is "anointed one," and in the context of Jewish history it's associated with "divine commission to a royal, priestly, or prophetic ministry." In time, it grew to refer specifically to the anointed one of God who would deliver Israel and usher in a kingdom of peace. By the time of Jesus, Jews viewed that coming *meshiah* as an incarnation of God himself.[4]

For Simon Peter to declare that Jesus was "the Messiah" meant more than simply adding a complimentary, descriptive title to his master. It was a declaration of belief in both the divinity and eternal sufficiency of Jesus. Peter was saying, in no uncertain terms, that the man Jesus was also God. In their intensely monotheistic Jewish society, that was blasphemy—and it was punishable by death (see Mark 14:61–64).

6. Peter said that Jesus is the Christ and the Son of God. What do you think that means?

7. What if Jesus were *not* God's son; would that make a difference to you? Explain.

8. In Matthew 16:17, Jesus says Peter is "blessed" by knowing who he really is. In what ways are we also blessed by knowing who Jesus really is?

## OPEN LIFE

9. Matthew 16:17 also suggests that not everyone will discover the truth about who Jesus is. Why do you think God has allowed you to know?

10. What's one thing from today's discussion you want to remember during the week to come? How will you help yourself remember it?

**Parent Tip**

Encourage family members to be specific in the way they answer "Open Life" questions. Also, allow kids to wait a minute or two in silence before answering. This will give them an opportunity to think through their responses a bit before having to talk about them.

# 30

# What Are You Waiting For?

"Follow me," Jesus told him, and Levi got up and followed him.

Mark 2:14

THEME: **Following Jesus**
SCRIPTURE: **Mark 2:13–17**

## OPEN UP

1. Let's plan a party! Other than the fact that it has to be in our home, the sky's the limit. What can we do to host the most awesome party ever?

2. Anybody we invite has promised to come to our awesome party. So whom will we invite?

**Parent Tip:** For Extra Fun

Plan a real party to celebrate your family's decision to follow Jesus. Invite friends and family from your church—and a few people from outside your church as well. Then have fun! Follow Jesus's example by being the kind of Christians that even non-Christians like to be around.

## OPEN BOOK

***Have family members read Mark 2:13–17.***

3. What's your impression of Levi after reading his story here? Explain.
4. After Levi decided to follow Jesus, something that looks a lot like a party broke out at his house. Why did that happen?
5. Levi was not the only disciple who dropped what he was doing to follow Jesus. How do you think those disciples would explain that decision to you?
6. We typically think of Jesus as having twelve disciples, but Mark 2:13–17 indicates that large crowds of people followed him around. What was so appealing about Jesus?

**Behind the Scenes:** Mark 2:14

Bible historians generally agree that the man identified as "Levi" in Mark 2:14 was actually the disciple we know today as Matthew—and the author of the Gospel that bears that name. The assumption is that he was called by two names, much as Peter was also called Simon.

Matthew's occupation as a tax collector would have been despised by his countrymen—and likely by Jesus's other disciples as well. In that day, the Romans allowed selected Jews to buy the right to collect transportation taxes from their fellow Hebrews. That arrangement most often resulted in corruption. Jewish tax collectors were known for demanding more payment than necessary and using that legalized extortion as a means toward personal wealth. Average Jews hated these collectors because they stole from their countrymen and supported the oppressive Roman government.[5]

7. What do you think it means for a kid to follow Jesus today? Describe it as if you were talking to your best friend.

8. Jesus invites all people to follow him. Some do and some don't. Why do you think that's so?

9. It sounds like Jesus was someone people liked to be around. Does that describe most Christians today? Why or why not?

## OPEN LIFE

10. What do you like about being near to Jesus? Explain.

11. What can we do to get closer to Jesus today? To help each other follow him all week long?

**Parent Tip**

Encourage family members to be specific in the way they answer "Open Life" questions. Also, allow kids to wait a minute or two in silence before answering. This will give them an opportunity to think through their responses a bit before having to talk about them.

# 31

# Good, Better, Best

Anyone who wants to be first must be the very last.

Mark 9:35

THEME: **Greatness**
SCRIPTURE: **Mark 9:33–36**

## OPEN UP

1. As of today, what are you greatest at?
2. If you could be known worldwide for one great accomplishment, what would you want it to be?

**Parent Tip:** For Extra Fun

Follow Jesus's example of caring for "the last" and have your family join you as volunteers in your church's nursery one week. Share responsibilities—and share Jesus's love with these littlest ones.

OPEN BOOK

3. Who do you think was the greatest of Jesus's disciples? Defend your choice.

*Have family members read Mark 9:33–36.*

4. Why were the disciples reluctant to tell Jesus what they had been discussing?

5. Jesus's definition of greatness was unexpected and hard to understand (see v. 35). If Jesus asked you to draw a picture for his disciples that would help explain what he meant, what would you put in your drawing?

**Behind the Scenes:** Mark 9:33–36

The disciples' argument over who was the greatest was likely an issue of rank, with several of them jockeying for more authority and privilege within Jesus's inner circle.

Jesus responded by telling his men that the first must be last in order to be great. The Greek word translated here as "first" is *protoi*, and it referred to "rulers, aristocrats, ruling priests, and other persons of authority and influence." The word referencing "last" (*eschatoi*) meant "to be someone with no rank, no authority, no privilege." Jesus emphasized his meaning by honoring, in front of his disciples, one of the *least* regarded members of society in that time: a child. In fact, simply listening to a child's chatter was considered beneath most people and a waste of time![6] Jesus, though, knew better—and wanted his disciples to know it as well.

6. Why is it so difficult to maintain a humble attitude?

7. Exactly how does serving others make someone great? Explain it.

8. In the time when Jesus and his disciples lived, children were not considered to be very important, so Jesus used a

child as an example of "the last." If he were here today, what might he use to demonstrate the same point?

## OPEN LIFE

9. Realistically, how can we become people who serve others well, even those we might consider "the last"? Let's brainstorm a list of ideas.

10. Which items from our list will we do as a family in the next month?

**Parent Tip**

Encourage family members to be specific in the way they answer "Open Life" questions. Also, allow kids to wait a minute or two in silence before answering. This will give them an opportunity to think through their responses a bit before having to talk about them.

# 32

# Easier Done than Said

I don't know this man you're talking about!
Mark 14:71

THEME: **Failure**
SCRIPTURE: **Mark 14:66–72**

## OPEN UP

1. Pretend you're one of Jesus's disciples from long ago. You've spent the past few years traveling, eating, and living with Jesus. What kinds of things have you experienced, and how have they changed you?
2. As a disciple, what's your favorite thing about Jesus?

**Parent Tip:** For Extra Fun

If your kids enjoy dress-up, it's fun to add Bible-time costumes to this family devotion. Use sheets for tunics and scarves for sashes, and add sandals to complete your ensembles!

## OPEN BOOK

***Have family members read Mark 14:66–72.***

3. What do you think the disciples felt when Jesus was arrested? How would you have felt?

4. By the time Mark 14:66–72 happened, Peter had watched Jesus get arrested by soldiers and he knew Jesus was being beaten and mocked by his accusers. Peter had to wonder if he was next. If you were Peter, what would you have done?

5. Denying Christ is known as Peter's greatest failure. If you were interviewing Peter about this incident for your school newspaper, what advice do you think he'd offer to you and your classmates?

**Behind the Scenes:** Mark 14:66–72

Of the eleven disciples left after Judas betrayed Jesus, only two were brave enough to follow Christ into the enemy's den. One was John; the other was Peter. The courtyard below the place where Jesus was being illegally tried and beaten was a legitimately dangerous place for Peter to be. It's no surprise then, that he was cowed into denying Jesus by a lowly servant girl. What is surprising is that the Bible records this cowardly behavior at all.

The classic historian Eusebius indicates that Mark's Gospel was first told to him by Peter himself.[7] The natural expectation would have been that Peter and Mark would downplay Peter's embarrassments and highlight his heroism instead. But just the opposite occurs here—and that actually adds to the credibility of the Gospel account. Theologians Mark Bailey and Tom Constable observe, "Mark's honesty in dealing with the failure of such a noted leader as Peter testifies to the veracity of Scriptures in revealing the failures and not just the successes of the early saints."[8]

6. When he realized what he had done, Peter wept. If you had been there, what would you have said to Peter right then?

7. After Peter denied him, do you think Jesus loved Peter more, less, or exactly the same? Defend your answer.

8. If Peter had chosen to live in shame because of his failure, how would that have affected his life—and ours?

## OPEN LIFE

9. When you fail, does Jesus love you more, less, or exactly the same? What difference does that make to you?

10. We all fail sometimes, and sometimes we are even hurtful to each other. What can we learn from Jesus and from Peter's experience to help us through those failures when they happen?

**Parent Tip**

Encourage family members to be specific in the way they answer "Open Life" questions. Also, allow kids to wait a minute or two in silence before answering. This will give them an opportunity to think through their responses a bit before having to talk about them.

# 33

# It's Just a *Little* Sin

For forty days he was tempted by the devil.
Luke 4:2

THEME: **Temptation**
SCRIPTURE: **Luke 4:1–13**

## OPEN UP

1. Close your eyes while I make the funniest face ever. Ready—go! Were you tempted to open your eyes to see my funny face? Why or why not?
2. Why do you think we're so often tempted to do things we know we shouldn't do?

**Parent Tip:** For Extra Fun

After this devotion, just for fun, why not have a Funniest Face Ever contest? Find a mirror somewhere and take turns, or use a digital camera to record your efforts. Award a standing ovation to everyone who participates!

## OPEN BOOK

***Have family members read Luke 4:1–13.***

3. There were no earthly witnesses to the encounter described in Luke 4:1–13, which means that Jesus must have told his followers about it later. Why do you suppose he felt it was important to share about this event with his disciples?

4. What if Jesus had given in to any of Satan's temptations? What do you think would have happened?

5. What are some ways that Satan tempts us to do wrong today?

**Behind the Scenes:** Luke 4:1–13

At the time of Jesus, the Jewish people had a few specific expectations about their coming Messiah. It's interesting to see that all of the temptations described in Luke 4 were ways for Jesus to prove—on Satan's terms—that he was the Messiah the world expected. Consider:

- Deuteronomy 18:15 promises a Messiah like Moses, God's prophet who gave the Israelites bread from heaven. Satan's first temptation, then, was a call for Jesus to demonstrate power like Moses and cause bread to miraculously appear.
- The Jewish Messiah was also expected to be a powerful political and military ruler here on earth.[9] Thus, Satan offered to make that expectation come true, offering Jesus all the kingdoms of the world—if only Christ would bow to him. Thankfully, Jesus refused!
- Additionally, many Jews in that time expected Christ to appear supernaturally in the sky. Theologian Herschel Hobbs reports, "The Jews thought of the Messiah as suddenly coming to his temple, perhaps floating down from its pinnacle amid

> the acclaim of the multitudes."[10] Satan's temptation, then, challenged Jesus to show he could do that. Jesus's response showed that the true Christ was much more than what men imagined he would be.

6. What advice would you give me if you knew I'd given in to temptation?

7. What advice would you want me to give you?

8. Whether they mean to be or not, friends are often the ones who tempt us to do wrong. How can you and I avoid being friends who tempt others to do wrong?

## OPEN LIFE

9. What can we learn from Jesus's example to help us the next time we face temptation at home, school, church, or anywhere else? Let's make a list.

10. When Satan tried to confuse and tempt him, Jesus used the Bible to help him remember what was really important. How can we help each other do the same this week?

> **Parent Tip**
>
> Encourage family members to be specific in the way they answer "Open Life" questions. Also, allow kids to wait a minute or two in silence before answering. This will give them an opportunity to think through their responses a bit before having to talk about them.

# 34

# Who's My Neighbor?

Which of these three do you think was a neighbor?
Luke 10:36

THEME: **Kindness**
SCRIPTURE: **Luke 10:25–37**

## OPEN UP

1. Let's have a Once-upon-a-Time Storyteller's Convention, right here, right now! Our theme for this convention is "kindness." What "once upon a time" stories can we make up that illustrate our theme?

2. What made it easy, or difficult, to make up a story about kindness?

**Parent Tip:** For Extra Fun

Try a Good Samaritan experiment sometime during the week after this devotion. Take your kids to a public place such as a grocery store, a mall, or a park. Ask your family to look around and spot

"Good Samaritan opportunities"—that is, opportunities to be kind to someone. Then try acting on those opportunities and see what happens. Be sure to talk about your experience afterward!

## OPEN BOOK

***Have family members read Luke 10:25–37.***

3. Instead of just giving a short answer to the question, "Who is my neighbor?" Jesus told a "once upon a time" story about kindness as his response. Why do you think he did that?

4. What are the important things you notice in Jesus's story? Tell about them.

5. In Jesus's society at that time, priests and Levites were admired as very religious people while Samaritans were not liked at all. Yet Jesus made a Samaritan the hero of this story. Why?

**Behind the Scenes:** Luke 10:25–37

Fast facts about Jesus's parable of the Good Samaritan:

- The road from Jerusalem to Jericho was about twenty-one miles long.
- This road typically was not used for commerce, but most often was traveled by religious pilgrims going to or from a religious festival.
- The road from Jerusalem to Jericho was well-known as a dangerous "neighborhood." The rocky terrain offered many hiding places for violent thieves to hide and then suddenly attack and rob unwary travelers.
- For safety's sake, religious pilgrims usually traveled in groups along this road rather than going it alone.
- In Jesus's parable, the priest, the Levite, and the Samaritan were each traveling alone, and therefore would have been at great risk to suffer the same fate as the man they saw bleeding and robbed on the side of the road.

- Priests and Levites were among the religious elite in Israel at this time, and would have been expected to act with mercy toward the injured man.
- In general, Samaritans and Jews hated each other much the same way as Arabs and Jews today are characterized as hating each other.
- Samaritans were considered enemies of both the Jews and God, and according to rabbinic teaching were not to be delivered from danger.
- The hated Samaritan, not the religious elite, was the one who showed God's mercy to another and thereby earned Jesus's approval as a "neighbor."[11]

6. What do the Samaritan's kind actions reveal about his personality?
7. What do our actions reveal about us to our friends and family members?
8. Why do you suppose Jesus thought it was so important for people to act with kindness and mercy toward each other?

## OPEN LIFE

9. What are specific ways we can follow the Samaritan's example in our daily lives? For instance, here in our home? At school? When we're out with friends? When we're grocery shopping? Wherever we are?
10. What if, every day this week, we prayed, "God, help me to be like the Good Samaritan"? What do you think would happen? Should we risk finding out?

**Parent Tip**

Encourage family members to be specific in the way they answer "Open Life" questions. Also, allow kids to wait a minute or two in silence before answering. This will give them an opportunity to think through their responses a bit before having to talk about them.

# 35

# Anywhere Prayer

When you pray, say: "Father. . . ."
Luke 11:2

THEME: **Prayer/National Day of Prayer**
SCRIPTURE: **Luke 11:1–4**

## OPEN UP

1. What are five words you'd use to describe prayer?
2. Why did you choose those words?

**Parent Tip:** For Extra Fun

Consider experiencing this devotion with your family on the National Day of Prayer in May. For more information and activities associated with this day, visit www.nationaldayofprayer.org.

OPEN BOOK

***Have family members read Luke 11:1–4.***

3. Why do you think the disciples wanted Jesus to describe prayer for them?

4. Do you think it's important that Jesus's model prayer begins by calling God our "Father"? Why or why not?

5. What does it mean to hallow, or honor, God's name? Tell me how we might do that today.

**Behind the Scenes:** Luke 11:1–4

According to theologian and Bible historian Timothy Paul Jones, there's one thing that makes the Lord's Prayer in Luke 11 different from any other prayer in history: the opening phrase, "Our Father." In the original Aramaic, the term for Father is *Abba*, and it "combined tender intimacy with profound respect." Here's how Dr. Jones describes it:

> Every child in Judea addressed her father as Abba, but no one ever addressed God this way. By commanding his disciples to pray "our Abba," Jesus was inviting them to enjoy the same intimate relationship with the Father that Jesus had experienced in eternity past. No parallel to these words exists in any other world religion. No Muslim would dream of addressing Allah as "our Abba"—Allah is powerful but not tender. No Hindu would consider calling the Brahmin "our Abba"—the divine life-force is universal but not personal. The Jews referred to God as "our Father" but never as "our Abba." "Our Abba" places the Lord's Prayer in a category by itself.[12]

6. "Daily bread" refers to our everyday needs like food and shelter. Why would Jesus tell us to ask God for ordinary things like that?

7. Forgiveness seems to be important to Jesus—so much so that he included it as a topic in his model prayer. What do you hear him saying to you and me about that?

8. What difference does it make, really, to pray for God to help us face temptation? Give examples.

## OPEN LIFE

9. Now that you've read Luke 11:1–4, how would you describe prayer to someone who was unfamiliar with it?

10. What are things you'd like us to pray about today? Let's do that now!

**Parent Tip**

Encourage family members to be specific in the way they answer "Open Life" questions. Also, allow kids to wait a minute or two in silence before answering. This will give them an opportunity to think through their responses a bit before having to talk about them.

# 36

# Who's Hungry?

Where shall we buy bread for these people to eat?
John 6:5

THEME: **God's Provision**
SCRIPTURE: **John 6:1–15**

## OPEN UP

1. If you could discover the secret to any magic trick, which one would you want to know?

2. Imagine you are an amazing magician and can cure any disease with just a wave of your hand—but you can only do it once. How will you use your great power?

**Parent Tip:** For Extra Fun

This devotion lends itself to mealtime, so consider enjoying a kid-friendly lunch with your family while you work through the discussion of John 6:1–15.

## OPEN BOOK

***Have family members read John 6:1–15.***

3. Jesus was not simply a magician doing tricks—he was a miracle worker changing real lives. If you'd been there and seen Jesus multiply five loaves and two fish into enough food to feed thousands of people, how would you have reacted?

4. Jesus could have said, "Okay, the show's over. Everybody go home." But instead he had everyone sit down for a free meal with him. Why did he do that?

5. Jesus's disciples had seen him heal the sick, cast out demons, and perform all kinds of other miracles, but apparently it never occurred to them that he could provide food for all those people. Why not?

**Behind the Scenes:** John 6:1–15

When Jesus multiplied loaves of bread to feed the five thousand, it meant something more than just a free lunch to those people. Just as Moses had miraculously provided bread in the wilderness, Jesus had now done the same, with great abundance. For the crowd gathered there, this was proof that Jesus was the Messiah that Moses prophesied about in Deuteronomy 18:15, "The LORD your God will raise up for you a prophet like me."

Almost immediately, the jubilant crowd moved to crown Jesus as king—by force. They assumed he was also a military leader who would overthrow their Roman rulers and usher in a new political dynasty in Israel. But that wasn't Christ's intention or desire, so he literally ran away from that temptation.[13] Interestingly, this is at least the second time Jesus turned down an opportunity to be an earthly king (see Luke 4:5–8). Our Messiah knew that his true kingdom was not of this world (see John 18:36).

6. What part did Jesus's followers play in bringing about this miracle of love and provision?

7. What part do we play today in helping to spread little miracles of God's love and provision?

8. What would have happened if that boy with the bread and fish had not been willing to share his lunch with God and others?

## OPEN LIFE

9. What are ways we can be like that little boy and share of ourselves with God and others?

10. What little miracles might happen if we did those things this next month? Should we risk finding out?

**Parent Tip**

Encourage family members to be specific in the way they answer "Open Life" questions. Also, allow kids to wait a minute or two in silence before answering. This will give them an opportunity to think through their responses a bit before having to talk about them.

# 37

# Dead-End Beginnings

I am the resurrection and the life.
John 11:25

THEME: **Death**
SCRIPTURE: **John 11:17–44**

## OPEN UP

1. What are your thoughts about death?

2. When someone dies, friends and family members gather at a funeral to comfort and support the people left behind. Whom would you want nearby at a funeral? Why?

**Parent Tip:** For Extra Fun

If the weather is nice, consider taking this discussion to a local cemetery or historical burial ground. Spend a little time exploring, reading interesting tombstones, and maybe even leaving flowers at a few graves. Then settle down somewhere and begin your devotion.

## OPEN BOOK

***Have family members read John 11:17–44.***

3. When Lazarus died, his sisters Mary and Martha wanted Jesus nearby to help comfort and support them—but Jesus waited four long days before arriving. How do you think the sisters felt while they waited for Jesus? Describe it—and show me that feeling on your face as well.

4. When Jesus finally got there, do you think Mary and Martha were relieved to see him, or upset that it took him so long to get there? Explain.

5. What do you think Mary and Martha thought about death?

**Behind the Scenes:** John 11:17, 39

It is significant that Jesus waited four days before coming to see his dead friend Lazarus. Rabbinic teaching proclaimed that death was irrevocable beyond three days, because by the fourth day the corpse had begun irreversible decay. The accepted belief was that after death a person's soul "hovers over the body, intending to reenter it. But as soon as it sees its appearance change [when decay sets in on the fourth day] it departs."[14]

By raising Lazarus after he'd been dead and buried for four days, Jesus did more than simply help a friend. He also made a definitive statement that he was God, with power over life, death, and eternity.

6. What did Jesus reveal about death to Mary and Martha? Why does that matter to us?

7. Jesus knew he would raise Lazarus, so why did he cry? What does this tell us about him?

8. From what you can tell, for whose sake did Jesus raise Lazarus? Defend your answer.

## OPEN LIFE

9. If you could ask Jesus anything about death, what would you want to know?

10. What does it mean to trust Jesus to be "the resurrection and the life" for us? How can that help us today, tomorrow, or a year from now?

**Parent Tip**

Encourage family members to be specific in the way they answer "Open Life" questions. Also, allow kids to wait a minute or two in silence before answering. This will give them an opportunity to think through their responses a bit before having to talk about them.

# 38

# Wow. Did You See That?

I have seen the Lord!
John 20:18

THEME: **Jesus's Resurrection/Easter**
SCRIPTURE: **John 20:1–18**

## OPEN UP

1. Would you rather have the ability to walk on water, the ability to walk through walls, or the ability to raise someone from the dead? Why?

2. Jesus did all three of those miracles. How do you think the disciples felt when they witnessed these amazing feats? Describe it.

**Parent Tip:** For Extra Fun

If your kids are the energetic and imaginative type, use couch cushions and pillows to create an "empty tomb" in your living room. Then have family members reenact John 20:1–18 as you read it aloud. This will be a fun way to help younger children picture in their minds the awesome events of that first Easter morning.

OPEN BOOK

***Have family members read John 20:1–18.***

3. When Jesus was killed, his disciples assumed that his miracles were over. So what do you think went through their minds when his tomb was discovered to be empty?

4. Mary, Peter, and John were the first ones to inspect the empty tomb. Then Peter and John left the tomb and returned home. Why did Mary stay?

5. After his resurrection, Jesus could have appeared to anyone at any time. Why do you think he chose to meet with Mary before anybody else?

**Behind the Scenes:** John 20:17

When Jesus appeared to Mary Magdalene after his resurrection, he gave what seemed like an odd command for Mary not to touch him. The classic King James Version translates this as "Touch me not," and today's New International Version renders it "Do not hold on to me." While both of those are adequate translations, neither appears to tell the full story. Pastor Chuck Swindoll offers clarification in context of the scene here. He says:

> The meaning of Jesus's gentle reproof is not immediately obvious, mostly because older translations have created undue confusion . . . the NASB more accurately renders the present tense, imperative command, "Stop clinging to Me." Mary felt so overwhelmed with relief—supposing she had her Lord back in the same manner as before—that she embraced Him and held on as though letting go would cause her to lose Him again.[15]

6. If you had been there with Mary when Jesus showed up, what would you have said to her? What would you have said to Jesus?

7. Why is it important for us to know that Jesus came back to life after he was dead and buried?

8. Some people didn't believe Mary was telling the truth, and they refused to believe Jesus had come back to life. Today some people still don't believe Mary's story or that Jesus came back to life. How do you think we should respond to those people?

## OPEN LIFE

9. If Jesus truly did come back to life on that first Easter Sunday, that means he is still alive today. How does that make you feel? Explain.

10. Jesus is alive! What difference will that make for you this week? Be specific.

**Parent Tip**

Encourage family members to be specific in the way they answer "Open Life" questions. Also, allow kids to wait a minute or two in silence before answering. This will give them an opportunity to think through their responses a bit before having to talk about them.

# 39

# Ain't No Thing

Who shall separate us from the love of Christ?
Romans 8:35

THEME: **God's Determined Love**
SCRIPTURE: **Romans 8:35–39**

## OPEN UP

1. What do you love? Let's make a list of at least twenty-five items!
2. When do you feel most like someone loves you? Let's make another list.

**Parent Tip:** For Extra Fun

Consider acting out some of the fun items on the list your family creates in answer to question 2. For instance, if someone mentions hugs, or foot rubs, or special songs, or whatever, go ahead and show that you love each other by doing those things right at that moment.

OPEN BOOK

***Have family members read Romans 8:35–39.***

3. In this passage Paul, the writer of Romans, made a list of a bunch of the crazy things that *cannot* separate us from Jesus's love. Why do you think he felt it was important to do that?

4. What would you add to Paul's list? Why?

5. Sometimes, when going through an unhappy time, we don't *feel* God's love. He might seem far away, or as if he doesn't see us or care about us. When do you feel like that?

**Behind the Scenes:** Romans 8:35–39

It's easy to view the grand declarations of Romans 8:35–39 as poetic utterances of truth—and they are that. But a glimpse at the times in which these words were written reveals forcefully that Paul's exhortations here were more than simply abstract, heavenly ideas. They reflected the bloody realities of daily Christian life. Consider: according to 2 Corinthians 11:23–28, Paul himself experienced personally and painfully all seven of the harsh events described in verse 35 (trouble, hardship, persecution, famine, nakedness, danger, violence of the sword). Additionally, Paul's readers were living in Rome during the bloody reign of Emperor Nero. In the days to come, this Roman Caesar would unleash hell on any and every follower of Christ he could find.[16] Yet even before Nero's great persecution, these Roman Christians faced torture and brutal death simply for believing in Jesus. One Bible historian describes their plight this way:

> In the early days of the church one or more Christians were martyred *every day*, or faced the possibility of it. Their

> persecutors valued Christians' lives as nothing more than animals to be butchered (italics mine).[17]

6. How might Romans 8:35–39 help us when we don't *feel* like God's love is near?

7. Romans 8:37 tells us that because of Jesus's love, we are "more than conquerors" in any situation. But really, what does that mean?

8. Finish this sentence: "I know for sure that God loves me because . . ." Explain your answer.

### OPEN LIFE

9. Jesus loves you—right here, right now. Why is that important to remember all the time?

10. What did you discover today that you would like to share with a friend this week?

> **Parent Tip**
>
> Encourage family members to be specific in the way they answer "Open Life" questions. Also, allow kids to wait a minute or two in silence before answering. This will give them an opportunity to think through their responses a bit before having to talk about them.

# 40

# Sincerely Yours

Love must be sincere.
Romans 12:9

THEME: **Healthy Friendships/Friendship Day**
SCRIPTURE: **Romans 12:9–21**

## OPEN UP

1. If today were International Cool Friends Day, what would we do to celebrate?
2. What qualities do you look for in a cool friend? Why?

**Parent Tip:** For Extra Fun

Friendship Day is an informal national holiday created by the United States Congress in 1935. It falls on the first Sunday of August each year. If your family is enjoying this devotion near or on that day, add in a few Friendship Day activities such as crafts, cooking, and more. Get fun ideas for your family at www.theholidayspot.com/friendship.

OPEN BOOK

*Have family members read Romans 12:9–21.*

3. How do the qualities described here compare to the qualities we look for in cool friends?

4. Finish this sentence: "When Romans 12:9 says 'Love must be sincere,' it means . . ." Explain your answer.

5. What happens when you or your friends don't follow the advice of Romans 12:16? What happens when you do?

**Behind the Scenes:** Romans 12:20

There is debate over what Paul means when he says that being kind to an enemy "will heap burning coals on his head." The apostle is clearly referring to a similar statement in Proverbs 25:21–22, but what exactly is he talking about?

Some commentators see this phrase as a metaphor for God's presence in judgment, repaying the evil person with his or her just punishment. In this view, the kindness of a Christian toward an enemy "increases the degree of judgment the enemy will receive." Other commentators, however, look to the context of this statement and feel that Paul is referring to a positive, hopeful outcome. In that view, the reference to "heaping coals" could refer back to an Egyptian ritual of repentance where a guilty person carried a bowl of hot coals on his head as a sign of change in his heart. Thus, Christian kindness could lead an enemy to repentance.[18]

6. When he wrote Romans 12:17–21, the apostle Paul seemed to be concerned about both the way we treat our friends and the way we treat our enemies. Why?

7. When is it easy to live out Paul's instructions in Romans 12? When is it hard?

8. What do you think is the most important advice Paul gives in Romans 12:9–21? Explain.

## OPEN LIFE

9. What would have to change for you to get better at being a "cool friend" like the one described in Romans 12:9–21?

10. With God's help, what can we do this week to start making that change?

**Parent Tip**

Encourage family members to be specific in the way they answer "Open Life" questions. Also, allow kids to wait a minute or two in silence before answering. This will give them an opportunity to think through their responses a bit before having to talk about them.

# 41

# Body Works

Now you are the body of Christ.
1 Corinthians 12:27

THEME: **The Church/Body of Christ**
SCRIPTURE: **1 Corinthians 12:12–27**

## OPEN UP

1. Who is the most important person you know? Defend your answer.

2. Finish this sentence: "I can tell that a person is important because . . ."

**Parent Tip:** For Extra Fun

Get out a biology book or check out a website like innerbody.com to find cool medical pictures of the human body and its various systems. Take time to marvel at the complexity and beauty of God's intricate creation, and use that as a reference point during today's discussion on the body of Christ.

OPEN BOOK

3. When do you feel unimportant? What makes you feel that way?

***Have family members read 1 Corinthians 12:12–27.***

4. According to what Paul says in 1 Corinthians 12:12–27, we're *all* important to each other because we're all part of Jesus's church. How would you explain that to someone who didn't believe it?

5. As a way of explaining why we're all important to each other, Paul compares Christians to the human body of Jesus. What does and does not make sense to you about that comparison?

**Behind the Scenes:** 1 Corinthians 12:12–27

In Paul's day, the city of Corinth in Greece was a major metropolitan area with more than a half million people living in it. It was a cosmopolitan place that put high social value on philosophy and religion. In fact, archaeologists have uncovered at least twelve competing temples to various Greek gods that were present in ancient Corinth.[19]

In this climate, the Christian church at Corinth became a place fractured by divisions and status seeking, particularly as it related to spiritual gifts. Bible historians believe that there had even arisen what we might call today a "cult of personality" around some gifted church leaders there. "Apparently the more spectacular gifts (such as tongues) had been glorified in the Corinthian church, making those who did not have them feel inferior."[20]

6. What else might be a good comparison to use when explaining Paul's message here?

7. If you have a pain in your foot, your whole body knows it. Paul says the same is true for the church. What does he mean by this? Can you give an example?

8. What would happen to the church if everyone was a mouth but no one was a hand?

## OPEN LIFE

9. If you had to pick a part of the body to describe where you think you fit in the church, what would you choose?

10. What's the most important thing you want to remember from today's discussion? How will you make sure to remember it this week?

**Parent Tip**

Encourage family members to be specific in the way they answer "Open Life" questions. Also, allow kids to wait a minute or two in silence before answering. This will give them an opportunity to think through their responses a bit before having to talk about them.

# 42

# Harvest Talk

Let us do good to all people.
Galatians 6:10

THEME: **Spiritual Growth/First Day of Autumn**
SCRIPTURE: **Galatians 6:7–10**

## OPEN UP

1. If you could, would you rather have a small money tree in the backyard or a large toys, games, and electronics garden in the front yard? Why?

2. If you could plant any small thing in the ground like a seed and have it grow into a larger version of the same thing, what would you want to plant?

**Parent Tip:** For Extra Fun

If time, weather, and location permit, this devotion is great to experience while outside in a garden or at a farm. Hanging out among the rows of a cornfield during the summer is especially fun, if that's an option for you and your family.

OPEN BOOK

*Have family members read Galatians 6:7–10.*

3. When he wrote this passage, the apostle Paul compared a person's spiritual growth and lifestyle to a garden. What do you think he was trying to say here? Explain it in your own words.

4. How does behaving badly toward others "grow" into bad consequences in our lives?

5. What happens when we do good to others? How does that "grow" into a good harvest for us?

**Behind the Scenes:** Galatians 6:7–9

The imagery of a harvest is used approximately one hundred times in Scripture, including Galatians 6:7–9. Though it seems outdated and a bit foreign to our high-tech culture today, the culture of Paul's readers was "a largely rural world of farming with its attendant sowing and harvesting. In that world, harvest is both an event of great annual importance and the preeminent image of abundance and reward for labor."

Additionally, Jewish religious feasts were often scheduled to occur during harvest time. For instance, Passover coincided with the barley harvest, Pentecost occurred at the time of the wheat harvest, and the Feast of Booths took place during the year-end fruit harvest. As such, the harvest symbol that Paul used would have been exciting for his readers, filled with associations of reward, generosity, blessing, and joy.[21]

6. How do we know whether or not our attitudes and actions are sowing "to please the Spirit" of God each day?

7. Sometimes it's hard to keep doing good. What makes you feel like giving up on planting good seeds in your life?

8. When you feel like giving up, what do you think Paul would want you to know? Tell me about it.

## OPEN LIFE

9. What do you think God wants you to learn about spiritual growth from our discussion today? Summarize it in one sentence.

10. What will you do differently this week because of that? What's one idea?

**Parent Tip**

Encourage family members to be specific in the way they answer "Open Life" questions. Also, allow kids to wait a minute or two in silence before answering. This will give them an opportunity to think through their responses a bit before having to talk about them.

# 43

# Powerful Weakness

The incomparable riches of his grace.

Ephesians 2:7

THEME: **Grace**

SCRIPTURE: **Ephesians 2:6–10**

## OPEN UP

1. If you were the owner of a detective agency, what kinds of secrets would you want your team to uncover?

2. Guess what? The Secret Detective Agency called, and they want to know the secret to living a Christian life. What should we tell them?

**Parent Tip:** For Extra Fun

When answering question 2, bring out your craft materials and make a "clue box" for the Secret Detective Agency. Include inside any mementos or reminders of kids' answers that might give "clues" to the agency as to what the secret is to living a Christian life. As the devotion continues, add new items (such as kids' definitions in answer to question 4) to the clue box. Keep the box in a prominent place during the week as a reminder of what you all learned through today's discussion.

## OPEN BOOK

***Have family members read Ephesians 2:6–10.***

3. If the Secret Detective Agency had called the apostle Paul (the author of Ephesians) for clues, what do you think he would have told them? Describe it in your own words.
4. How would you define the word *grace*?

**Parent Tip**

If your children are not yet Christians, this devotion can be an opportunity to help them begin their own relationship with Jesus. Feel free to expand on the discussion in response to questions 5 and 6 to include a summary of the gospel, and to invite your children to receive God's saving grace in their lives today.

5. In what ways is God's grace the secret to a Christian life? Describe them.
6. What do you think is an appropriate response to God's grace in our lives?

**Behind the Scenes:** Ephesians 2:8

The Greek word translated as "grace" in Ephesians 2:8 is *charis*. According to Bible scholar Lawrence Richards, "It means a gracious favor or benefit bestowed, and at the same time it means the gratitude appropriate to the grace received. . . . The concept came to include both gracious action and agreeable human qualities."

The apostle Paul took that word one step further. Says Richards, "Paul fastened on *charis* to communicate the truth that lies at the heart of God's saving work in Jesus. To Paul, grace is a transforming reality. . . . It transforms our present and eternal destiny. . . . It is the triumphant announcement that God in Christ has acted and come to the aid of all who will trust him."[22]

In short, *charis* changes everything . . . forever.

7. Why are we sometimes forgetful or ungrateful when it comes to God's grace?

8. Ephesians 2:10 tells us that we are God's handiwork, created to do good works. How does God's grace help us so that we can do that?

## OPEN LIFE

9. What makes it difficult sometimes for Christians to share God's grace with others?

10. What's one thing about God's grace that makes you feel grateful? Let's thank God for that now.

**Parent Tip**

Encourage family members to be specific in the way they answer "Open Life" questions. Also, allow kids to wait a minute or two in silence before answering. This will give them an opportunity to think through their responses a bit before having to talk about them.

# 44

# All Dressed Up

Clothe yourselves with compassion.
Colossians 3:12

THEME: **Loving Lifestyle**
SCRIPTURE: **Colossians 3:12–17**

## OPEN UP

1. Superman, Batman, or Wonder Woman . . . whom would you rather have as your best friend? Why?
2. What are the best qualities to look for in a close friend?

**Parent Tip:** For Extra Fun

If your kids are the dramatic type, send everyone to their respective rooms with instructions to return in five minutes wearing the best superhero costumes they can create from stuff in the house. Applaud their efforts—and join in the fun! Then go through this devotion as your very own superfamily.

**OPEN BOOK**

3. What is it about you that makes you a "super" friend?

***Have family members read Colossians 3:12–17.***

4. How do the virtues identified here compare with the qualities we admire in a close friend? What's similar, and what's different?

5. Colossians 3:14 points out that love is the most important virtue in a person. How do you see that coming true in real life?

**Behind the Scenes:** Colossians 3:15

When Paul encouraged his readers in Colossae to "let the peace of Christ rule in your hearts," it was an appeal to their competitive sensibilities. The word used for "rule" here is *brabeuō*, an athletic term that refers to the umpire or official judge of a sporting game or conflict between opposing athletes.

In Colossae, these Christians were often faced with danger and even demonic oppression. Instead of letting fear rule their lives and actions, Paul reminded them—and us—that Christ's promised peace has ruled in our favor. We, like the Colossians, can choose to trust that peace to *brabeuō* over any opposition to our faith, over any circumstance, no matter how overpowering it may seem to be at first.[23]

6. Colossians 3:12–17 could be summarized as "a loving lifestyle." In what ways does this passage also describe Jesus and his loving lifestyle? Give examples.

7. True or false: "When I live a loving lifestyle, I show Jesus to people around me." Defend your answer.

8. What makes it hard to live a loving lifestyle here in our home? Outside of our home?

## OPEN LIFE

9. What might help us to live a loving lifestyle, even when it's hard? Let's brainstorm ideas.

10. If you and I were determined to live out Colossians 3:17 all day tomorrow, what would that look like? How can we make that happen?

**Parent Tip**

Encourage family members to be specific in the way they answer "Open Life" questions. Also, allow kids to wait a minute or two in silence before answering. This will give them an opportunity to think through their responses a bit before having to talk about them.

# 45

## Lucy, He's Ho-ome!

The Lord himself will come down from heaven.
1 Thessalonians 4:16

THEME: **Jesus's Return**
SCRIPTURE: **1 Thessalonians 4:13–18**

### OPEN UP

1. What if you had the power to bring back anyone from history for one hour? Whom would you want to meet? Why?
2. What if you could peek into the future on your television set? What great event would you want to witness? Describe it.

**Parent Tip:** For Extra Fun

After this devotion, pull out stationery and markers, and create a few encouragement cards based on 1 Thessalonians 4:13–18. Mail them to friends and leaders at your church. Then you'll actually be following the instructions of verse 18 in this passage!

OPEN BOOK

***Have family members read 1 Thessalonians 4:13–18.***

3. When Jesus returns, it'll be like bringing back someone from history *and* like seeing an awesome event from the future. How would you describe that moment to someone who might be watching you on television right now?

4. Why is it important for us to know that Jesus is coming again?

5. Nobody knows the exact day when Jesus will return. Why do you think God has planned it that way?

**Behind the Scenes:** 1 Thessalonians 4:13, 15

Acts 17:1–10 reveals that when Paul first planted the church in Thessalonica, he actually caused a riot! In fact, he was forced to sneak away by night to protect the fledgling body of believers from persecution. As a result, he likely didn't have time to teach this church more than just the barest essentials about Jesus's second coming. When some in the Thessalonian church died, the remaining believers worried about their eternal fate. Paul wrote to assuage their fears and to share the hopeful promise of Jesus's return for all believers, dead and alive.

In 1 Thessalonians 4:15, Paul states clearly that this teaching came directly from Jesus himself, leading many to ask the question of how Paul heard Christ speak this. There are four theories: (1) this theology came from a teaching of Jesus that's not recorded in the Gospel accounts; (2) it's a paraphrase of Jesus's teachings about the end times, as recorded in Mark 13 and Matthew 24; (3) it's a general summary of Jesus's overall teaching; or (most likely) (4) Jesus spoke this supernaturally to Paul, much as he did when he spoke to Paul on the road to Damascus (see Acts 9).[24]

6. Jesus is going to make a big entrance when he returns, with angels, trumpets, and a great shout. What's the purpose of that?

7. The apostle Paul expected Jesus to return before he died—but that didn't happen. Does that mean Paul was wrong when he wrote 1 Thessalonians 4:13–18? Explain your answer.

8. Do you think it makes a difference whether or not you believe Jesus will return in your lifetime? Why or why not?

## OPEN LIFE

9. First Thessalonians 4:18 tells us to encourage each other with the news of Jesus's future return. How does that encourage us?

10. What do you think it means to "be ready" for Jesus to come again? How can you and I "be ready" this week?

**Parent Tip**

Encourage family members to be specific in the way they answer "Open Life" questions. Also, allow kids to wait a minute or two in silence before answering. This will give them an opportunity to think through their responses a bit before having to talk about them.

# 46

# Book People

All Scripture is God-breathed.
2 Timothy 3:16

THEME: **The Bible**
SCRIPTURE: **2 Timothy 3:14–17**

## OPEN UP

1. What is something you carry with you all the time? (For instance, a purse? A wallet? Lip balm?)
2. What if your Bible were as "joined at the hip" with you as that item is? What would be different for you?

**Parent Tip:** For Extra Fun

Bring a few highlighters to share during this devotion. As part of the answer to question 7, give a highlighter to each child. Encourage them to spotlight verses of Scripture they think are important or meaningful, and which they'll want to remember later. For instance, your kids might start today by highlighting 2 Timothy 3:16 in their own Bibles.

## OPEN BOOK

3. When is the first time you remember God using the Bible to speak an important message to you? What happened?

***Have family members read 2 Timothy 3:14–17.***

4. What do you see here that's important? Explain it.
5. Exactly how does the Bible do all the things listed in verse 16? Give examples.

**Behind the Scenes:** 2 Timothy 3:16

Paul states in 2 Timothy 3:16 that all Scripture is "God-breathed" (or "inspired by God," in some translations). Pastor Chuck Swindoll sheds light on that terminology by saying, "The phrase is rendered from a single word that combines *theos*, 'God,' and the verb *pneō*, 'to breathe.'"

This "God-breathed" imagery is significant in that it clearly draws a comparison between the creation of Scripture and the awe-inspiring creation of the first man and woman. Genesis 2:7 reveals that God formed the first human, Adam, from the "dust of the ground"—but Adam did not actually *live* until God breathed life into him. Before that God-breath, Adam was what Swindoll calls "organized dirt." Likewise, words of Scripture are more than just "organized ink." As Pastor Swindoll observes, "Only God-breathed words possess His life."[25]

6. If 2 Timothy 3:17 is true, then you have the power to fulfill any good work God wants you to do. How does that make you feel?
7. How does someone like you or me use the Bible to experience what's described in 2 Timothy 3:14–17? Explain it

as though you're speaking to someone who has never seen a Bible before.

8. Some people say, "The Bible isn't really for kids." Do you agree or disagree? Defend your answer.

### OPEN LIFE

9. Why is it important to know, and believe, that the words of the Bible are from God?

10. What will you remember from today's devotion that might help you during the coming week at school? At home? When hanging out with friends?

**Parent Tip**

Encourage family members to be specific in the way they answer "Open Life" questions. Also, allow kids to wait a minute or two in silence before answering. This will give them an opportunity to think through their responses a bit before having to talk about them.

# 47

# Faith Is . . .

Now faith is confidence in what we hope for.
Hebrews 11:1

THEME: **Faith**
SCRIPTURE: **Hebrews 11:1**

## OPEN UP

1. Finish this sentence: "Before today is over, I really hope that . . ." Explain your answer.
2. Finish this sentence: "Before my life is over, I have faith that . . ." Explain your answer.

**Parent Tip:** For Extra Fun

To illustrate some of the discussion in answer to questions 3–5, try a "Family Trust Fall" exercise. Have one person fall backward into the outstretched arms of the rest of the family. Then ask how he or she would explain the difference between *hoping* the family would make the catch and *knowing* the family would make the catch.

OPEN BOOK

***Have family members read Hebrews 11:1.***

3. Hebrews 11:1 tells us that faith is not hope, but being sure of hope. What's the difference?
4. What happens when people have faith in things that are not true?
5. How do we decide what deserves our faith and what doesn't? Give examples.

**Behind the Scenes:** Hebrews 11:1

The Greek word used in Hebrews 11:1 for "confidence in" (or "assurance" or "substance," in some translations) is *hupŏstasis.* This word encompassed more than simply the abstract essence of faith. Rather, *hupŏstasis*—substance—in this context is also a physical, solid thing. It means literally "a setting under (support)."[26] In other words, faith (an abstract concept) is best described as a concrete object, such as a table or load-bearing support beam or even the foundation of a house, that holds up firmly under the weight of another concrete object.

To some, faith is easily confused as a synonym for hope, or as positive imagination or unseen potential. But to those who grasp the true nature of *hupŏstasis* and apply it to life, authentic faith is much more than that. Like the unseen foundation of a house, faith is the hidden *substance* of very real truth, the often invisible reality that holds up the smaller, partly perceived hopes of our daily lives.

6. Hebrews 11:1 tells us that through faith we can be "certain of what we do not see." How does that work?
7. What does faith in Jesus mean to you? Describe it.

8. Sometimes bad things happen to good people. How does faith in Jesus help us to understand and deal with situations like that?

## OPEN LIFE

9. What do you think God's hopes are for you?

10. How can your faith in Jesus help you pursue God's hopes for you this week? Give examples.

**Parent Tip**

Encourage family members to be specific in the way they answer "Open Life" questions. Also, allow kids to wait a minute or two in silence before answering. This will give them an opportunity to think through their responses a bit before having to talk about them.

# 48

# The Say-Do System

Do not merely listen to the word.
James 1:22

THEME: **Faith-Filled Lifestyle**
SCRIPTURE: **James 1:22–25**

## OPEN UP

1. There's a new reality television show called *Who's the Christian Anyway?* To win, you've got to identify the undercover Christian on the show. How will you figure it out?
2. Generally speaking, do you think it's easy or difficult to spot Christians in real life? Why?

**Parent Tip:** For Extra Fun

As part of your discussion during question 9, consider creating "Hearer and Doer!" awards to give as encouragement to the people you identify. Share them with your chosen people sometime in the next week.

OPEN BOOK

***Have family members read James 1:22–25.***

3. If we were on the *Who's the Christian Anyway?* television show, and we followed the instructions of James 1:22–25, do you think it would be easy or difficult for people to tell that we're Christians? Why?

4. James says people who "merely listen" to God's Word are deceiving themselves. What does he mean?

5. How does a person actually do what God's Word says? Give examples.

**Behind the Scenes:** James 1:23–24

Unlike in our modern society, mirrors were not a common part of a typical household in the ancient Middle East—and even when they were they couldn't produce anything close to the image accuracy that we're accustomed to today. In wealthier families, mirrors were used primarily as a helpful tool for hairstyling. Most likely, though, James's reference in 1:23–24 is to the general public, who had only occasional access to a mirror and might be more inclined to forget their outward appearance from day to day.

Either way, the implication of James's statement is not complimentary! In the case of wealthy folks, James's words would be insulting, picturing them as stupid and absent-minded. In reference to an average person, James's characterization would suggest that person was shallow and forgetful. His point is clear: God's Word is a valuable tool, and we're foolish if we apply it carelessly or infrequently in our lives.[27]

6. James is kind of insulting toward people who hear God's Word but don't live it out, comparing them to idiots who can't

even remember what they look like (see James 1:23–24). Do you think that insult is fair? Why or why not?

7. James also indicates that the person who lives out God's Word in his or her lifestyle receives blessings from God (see v. 25). What kinds of blessings do you think he means?

8. What makes it difficult sometimes to live out the Christian faith? What can we do about that?

## OPEN LIFE

9. Who is one person you know that, as far as you can tell, seems to be living out the wisdom of James 1:22–25? Tell about that person.

10. What can we learn from that person and from James 1:22–25 to help us to more openly live out our faith in Jesus this week?

**Parent Tip**

Encourage family members to be specific in the way they answer "Open Life" questions. Also, allow kids to wait a minute or two in silence before answering. This will give them an opportunity to think through their responses a bit before having to talk about them.

# 49

# Tame That Tongue!

Anyone who is never at fault in what they say is perfect.

James 3:2

THEME: **Self-Control**
SCRIPTURE: **James 1:26; 3:2–10**

## OPEN UP

1. Think of your favorite song. Can you sing it without using your tongue? Try right now!
2. How about this: Can you say this tongue twister five times fast? "Irish wristwatch." Try it!

**Parent Tip:** For Extra Fun

There are many well-known sayings about guarding what we say. "Actions speak louder than words," "If you can't say anything nice, don't say anything at all," and "A gentle word turns away wrath" are just a few. Encourage your kids to choose a common saying (or a Bible verse) that'll help them remember to be careful with their words. Then have everyone write down their sayings and carry them along as they go through the coming week.

**OPEN BOOK**

***Have family members read James 1:26; 3:2–10.***

3. Imagine that you woke up this morning without a tongue. What will you miss most while living as a tongueless wonder?

4. Your tongue is powerful; some say it's the strongest muscle in your body. What do you hear James saying about the power of your tongue in these verses? Summarize it in your own words.

5. In this passage, James uses several different comparisons to describe the power of the tongue. Which one seems most accurate to you? Explain.

**Behind the Scenes:** James 3:2

When James wrote the words, "We all stumble in many ways" in James 3:2, it's entirely likely he was thinking of his own life and the slander he once spoke about Jesus.

Bible scholars generally agree that the author of this epistle was most likely Jesus's half brother James, who eventually became the preeminent leader of the Jerusalem church.[28] But before that, the second son of Mary and Joseph grew up in the shadow of a real "perfect" older brother! Like others in his family, James was skeptical of Jesus's claims to divinity. John 7:1–5 reveals that Jesus's brothers, with James likely leading them, mocked Christ at least once, and tried to goad him into foolish action. Even more damning, Mark 3:21 records a time when Mary's family—again, with James likely in the lead—declared publicly that their Jesus was actually insane.

So when James wrote his warnings about taming the tongue, he may have been thinking about his own failings in that area—and the way he once let his tongue insult his own Savior.

6. Fire and poison are two words used to describe the hurtful effects of ill-spoken words. When have you felt like someone's words hurt you like fire or poison? What did you do?

7. What do the things we say reveal about who we are inside?

8. In James 3:9–10, James seems really bothered that our mouths can both bless God and curse men. Why is that such a big deal?

## OPEN LIFE

9. When is it hardest for you to control your tongue?

10. If he were here right now, what advice do you think James would give us about those situations? Let's try to follow that advice this week!

**Parent Tip**

Encourage family members to be specific in the way they answer "Open Life" questions. Also, allow kids to wait a minute or two in silence before answering. This will give them an opportunity to think through their responses a bit before having to talk about them.

# 50

# Love Like You Mean It

Let us love one another, for love comes from God.
1 John 4:7

THEME: **Love/Valentine's Day**
SCRIPTURE: **1 John 4:7–12**

## OPEN UP

1. Brach's candy company called: they need new slogans for this year's candy hearts! What ideas can we give them?
2. Even worse, Cupid has resigned. He's tired of flying around in a diaper and is ready to move on in his professional career. Who should take over as the mascot for Valentine's Day?

**Parent Tip:** For Extra Fun

Well, it seems almost too obvious, but as a special treat to go along with this devotion, go ahead and get your family some of those conversation hearts to share. Pick out special sayings for each of your kids (for instance, "U rock!" or "U R sweet") and present the appropriate heart candy with a hug and a compliment for your child.

OPEN BOOK

3. Besides giving a card or candy on Valentine's Day, how do people in our family show that we love each other? Give examples.

*Have family members read 1 John 4:7–12.*

4. Love is more than just a holiday slogan—it's the heart of who God is! What are five important things you hear John saying about love in these verses? Why do you think those are important?

5. Love comes from God (see v. 7). What does that kind of love look like? Describe it.

**Behind the Scenes:** 1 John 4:9–10

John's message that God is the initiator of love toward us would have been hard for many of the more religious Jews in ancient Palestine to accept. Perhaps that's why he emphasized it so strongly, and with repetition, in 1 John 4:9–10!

According to Jewish theological sources extant in that time, many held a more legalistic perspective that dictated one must earn God's love; it was not freely given. For instance, one group known as the Therapeutae viewed God's love as the "appropriate reward" for a virtuous lifestyle. Others preached that God would love you only if you took care of orphans. Or that God would deign to love you if you visited the sick and performed good deeds.[29]

But John set the record straight on this matter: God loved us before we could ever do anything that might presume to earn that love—and he proved it by sending his Son Jesus to redeem us from our sins.

6. When we love others, we're spreading God's love. How does that work during a normal day in your life?

7. In what ways does God's love change you and me for the better?

8. What if God only liked us, but didn't love us? Would that make anything different? Explain.

## OPEN LIFE

9. What if we only liked God, but didn't love him? Would that make any changes in the way we act toward God?

10. How can we show God this week that we love him? Let's brainstorm ideas!

**Parent Tip**

Encourage family members to be specific in the way they answer "Open Life" questions. Also, allow kids to wait a minute or two in silence before answering. This will give them an opportunity to think through their responses a bit before having to talk about them.

# 51

# True or False?

[Build] yourselves up in your most holy faith.
Jude 1:20

THEME: **Truth**
SCRIPTURE: **Jude 1:17–25**

## OPEN UP

1. True or false: you can trust everything a church leader or teacher tells you. Defend your answer.

2. How do you know if someone is telling the truth about God?

**Parent Tip:** For Extra Fun

If your kids are the musical type—or just enjoy being creative—use Jude 1:24–25 as a catalyst for a family music time. Encourage everyone to work together to invent a new song that uses part or all of these verses as the lyrics. Beat-box sound effects and hip-hop dance moves are optional!

OPEN BOOK

***Have family members read Jude 1:17–25.***

3. Jude wrote this letter to warn Christians because some of their leaders weren't telling the truth about God. Do you think we still need this kind of warning today? Why or why not?

4. Jude suggests that we can avoid being deceived by false teachers by building ourselves up in our "most holy faith" (see v. 20). What's he talking about here?

5. What do you think we should do when we hear someone teaching something untrue about God?

**Behind the Scenes:** Jude 1:17–19

Bible scholar Warren Wiersbe observes, "Wherever there is the authentic, the counterfeit will appear."[30] Apparently this was also true at the time Jude was written.

Previously, the apostle Peter had written to these churches with a warning about false teachers who would infiltrate their ranks and lead many astray (see 2 Peter 2:1–3). Jude now sees that prophetic warning coming true, and writes as a follow-up to Peter's letter. A group of false teachers had arisen who were "exploitative promoters of unrestrained sexual immorality," and they were now harmfully influencing several churches.[31]

To combat their influence, Jude points his readers back to one of the key tools for discerning whether or not a teacher speaks truth about Christ: "Remember what the apostles of our Lord Jesus Christ foretold" (Jude 1:17). Wiersbe explains, "Since Christ had committed 'the faith' (Jude 3) to His Apostles . . . Apostolic teaching was, and still is, the test of truth."[32]

6. Sometimes people just get confused and don't know what to believe about God—and sometimes that may even

happen to you and me. What can we learn from verses 21–23 to help us in those situations?

7. The words of Jude 1:24–25 have actually been sung as a worship song for many centuries. In one sentence, what would you say is Jude's main message in these verses?

8. Why is that message important for us today?

## OPEN LIFE

9. If Jude were to hang out with you tomorrow, what advice do you think he'd give you?

10. This week as we go through our everyday lives, how can we follow the good advice we gained from Jude 1:17–25?

**Parent Tip**

Encourage family members to be specific in the way they answer "Open Life" questions. Also, allow kids to wait a minute or two in silence before answering. This will give them an opportunity to think through their responses a bit before having to talk about them.

# 52

# What's Up?

There before me was a door standing open in heaven.
Revelation 4:1

THEME: **Heaven**
SCRIPTURE: **Revelation 4:1–11**

## OPEN UP

1. What do you know about heaven? Tell me your thoughts.
2. What do you think would happen if you were invited to visit heaven for an hour or so? Describe it.

**Parent Tip:** For Extra Fun

If you have time and creative energy at the end of this devotion, grab some sidewalk chalk and head out to your driveway or a sidewalk in front of your home. Invite each family member to use the chalk to draw a picture that illustrates one element of the scene described in Revelation 4:1–11. For instance, someone might draw an emerald rainbow, a colorful throne, one of the "living creatures," and so on.

When you're done, you'll have a sidewalk mural of Revelation 4:1–11 to remind you of your family devotion today!

OPEN BOOK

3. If you were the host of a television program and you had a guest on your show who'd spent an hour in heaven, what would you ask that person? Why?

***Have family members read Revelation 4:1–11.***

4. Believe it or not, the apostle John actually did get a glimpse of heaven. What comes to your mind after reading his description of it in Revelation 4:1–11?

5. In John's view of heaven, God sits on a great throne as king of everything. How does that make you feel? Why?

**Behind the Scenes:** Revelation 4:2–3

John's vision of "a throne in heaven with someone sitting on it" is consistent with other prophetic views of God in his heavenly glory (see Isa. 6:1). The description of God and his heavenly throne in terms of precious stones of rainbow colors is also consistent with previous biblical visions (see Ezek. 1:28).

In choosing gemstones (jasper, carnelian, and emeralds) as comparative images for heaven's inexplicable sights, John's descriptive choices would easily be recognized by his readers as highly valued objects. Carnelian (a translucent red gemstone) was particularly admired, as it was used in Greek and Roman jewelry.[33]

6. The four "living creatures" sound like special effects from a movie! But they are real, and they are constantly near

God. If they came over for dinner one night, what do you think they'd tell us about God?

7. The most important thing about heaven is that God is there. The most important thing about life here on earth is that God is here too. Why does that make a difference for us?

8. Sometimes we can see a little bit of heaven here on earth—like in the beauty of the sky, the kindness of a friend, or even the deliciousness of our food. How have you seen a little bit of heaven on earth this past week?

## OPEN LIFE

9. Why do you think heaven is filled with people and creatures who are constantly saying how wonderful God is?

10. What's one thing you know about God that's wonderful? When was the last time you told him that? Let's talk to God about that right now.

**Parent Tip**

Encourage family members to be specific in the way they answer "Open Life" questions. Also, instruct kids to wait a minute or two in silence before answering. This will give them an opportunity to think through their responses a bit before having to talk about them.

# Appendix

## *Twenty Tips for Fantastic Family Discussions*

**1. Relax.**

When leading devotions, some parents get a little stressed and feel pressure to do a "good" job. Often, this translates into strained discussions, kids who feel uncomfortable, and parents who feel like failures. So you know what? Forget about all that stuff. Just relax. Be yourself. Start the conversation and see where it takes you. Let God worry about the rest.

**2. Enjoy yourself!**

Your children will follow your example during family devotion time. If you are stern and serious and can't crack a smile, they'll end up hating the study of God's Word. So why not enjoy yourself? Hey, you're hanging out with your kids and talking about God—two of the coolest things on earth! Laugh a little. Be flexible. Be creative. Have fun! If you have a good time, your kids will have a good time—and everyone will benefit.

**3. Challenge your kids to think beyond the obvious.**

Our children are socially trained to try to give us the "right" answer when we ask a question. That means a lot of kids will offer "Jesus!" or some other safe response when you try to spark a discussion.

Don't reprimand them for that—but do challenge your family to avoid easy, risk-free answers and to dig deeper. And let them know that not everything has a "right" answer, so they have the freedom to brainstorm new ideas—even if it means raising more questions.

**4. Use follow-up cues.**

When challenging your kids to think beyond the obvious, it can be helpful to use follow-up cues to help them go deeper. For instance, if a child offers a simple statement or a one-sentence response, try saying something like: "Tell me more about that," "What do you mean?" "How would you explain that to your little sister?" "That's interesting; help me understand it more," "What else?" or "Defend your answer." You get the idea.

**5. Make it okay for there to be occasional silence.**

Hey, it takes time to think about things that are important, so let your kids have that time. Don't give in to the temptation to fill silences when thinking is occurring. Just wait for your family members to work through their thoughts. Somebody will speak up soon enough.

**6. Remember, there's rarely one "right" answer.**

Look, if this were a Bible quiz book then you could expect there to be a single "correct" answer to every question. But that's lower-order thinking. This book, however, is all about getting your kids to move toward higher-order thinking about the Bible. That means anything's possible once a question is out there. Get used to it. You might like it.

**7. Resist the temptation to be the Answer King (or Queen).**

Sometimes children will look to you to provide clues as to what you want them to say, or even to deliver the "right" answer to a discussion question. Avoid the temptation to fill in that blank for them. Instead, help your kids think for themselves about God's Word by holding back your natural tendency to deliver instruction. When they ask you to define some aspect of a question, say, "What do you think about that? You decide." When they want you to deliver a definitive answer, say, "How would you answer that if you were me?" Remember, when they talk, they learn—so get out of the way whenever you can.

**8. Get comfortable with saying, "I don't know."**

This is related to the whole Answer King (or Queen) thing, but worth noting separately. Sometimes your kids will ask a question you just don't feel comfortable answering. Don't try to bluff your way through it; just be honest and say something like, "I don't really know the answer to that question. What do you think we could do to help us find an answer?" Your kids will like knowing that you are joining them on their journey of discovery.

**9. Remember, a family devotion is first and foremost a conversation.**

Because you'll be studying the Bible as a family, it'll be tempting to fall into teacher/student roles. Try to remember that school is the place for teachers and students; your home is the place for faith *conversations*. Let your time together be one of give-and-take, of friends chatting and enjoying a good discussion about God's Word.

**10. Be consistent.**

One of the greatest tools in family devotions is simple: consistency. Children respond to routine; it gives them a sense of security and communicates through actions what you say your life values are. So plan to have your family gather to discuss God's Word on a regular schedule. For instance, maybe you'll spend a half hour every Tuesday night in family devotions. Or maybe you'll have devotions on the first Sunday of every month. Choose what works best for your family—and then stick to it.

**11. Be flexible.**

Ha! After reading tip number ten above, you probably think we're giving you the exact opposite advice here, right? Wrong. What we're saying is that, once you've established a familiar pattern for your family devotions, it's okay to throw in a few surprises from time to time. For instance, why not have a family devotion during a car trip to visit relatives? Or what if you invite another family to enjoy a devotion with yours? Be creative, be flexible, and have fun.

**12. Be real.**

If the only time you ever talk about God and the Bible with your kids is during a family devotion, then that's a problem. The expectation is that you, the parent, are not only leading children closer to God, but also are continually growing in your own relationship with Jesus. Let that reality show in your daily life and conversations with your children. If they see you on Wednesday living out—and talking about—what you all learned during your devotion on Sunday, that kind of authenticity will stay with them for a lifetime.

**13. Pay attention to where you hold your family devotions.**

Kids who are physically uncomfortable soon become emotionally and intellectually uncomfortable. So plan to meet somewhere with comfortable seating, few distractions, pleasant temperatures, and so on. Why sit stiff-backed at the dining room table when that comfy living room couch is just in the other room? Let your kids sprawl and relax while you chat, and it'll communicate to them that talking about God is a normal part of life.

**14. Encourage your kids to ask questions.**

A good Bible discussion follows an outline, but never a script. Sometimes the questions you ask will prompt more questions from your family members. That's okay—it shows they're thinking about the topic. So welcome relevant questions from your kids, and sometimes even ask for them.

**15. Make the discussion questions work for you, not vice versa.**

As you work through the discussion guides in *Instant Family Devotions*, you'll soon discover that the order of the questions does follow a progression. However, that doesn't mean you have to ask every question in order. Feel free to adapt the questions, and the question order, to fit your family's interests and experience—and to add all-new questions of your own.

**16. Remember, it's okay if you don't finish an entire discussion guide.**

Sometimes a single question can spark enough conversation to fill half an hour. Other times, a question may seem to fall flat with your family. Those things are both okay. If kids seem interested and talkative about a certain aspect of a devotion, go with the flow and let the conversation go on. If a question doesn't seem to fit with your family, go ahead and skip it and move to the next one.

Follow your family's lead and focus on the questions that seem most relevant and compelling, even if that means leaving a question or two out of the discussion.

**17. Let your kids be the leaders sometimes.**

One great thing about *Instant Family Devotions* is that anyone can lead. So, from time to time, go ahead and let someone else lead! Start the devotion, then toss the book to one of your kids and have him or her take a turn facilitating discussion time. That kind of thing builds camaraderie and confidence—and communicates that you value and respect your kids.

**18. Try the "For Extra Fun" tips.**

Every devotion in this book has a simple, creative idea to add a little extra fun to your family's experiences when studying the Bible. Find the ones that seem appropriate for your kids and go ahead and try them out. Chances are you'll all enjoy these easy add-on ideas.

**19. Pray.**

The best family devotion in the world is irrelevant if God is not at work. And the most innocuous conversation can change a person forever—if God is at work. So be sure to take time (before, during, after) to pray for God to be at work in the hearts and lives of your family members. You'll definitely notice the difference!

**20. Trust!**

It's hard to believe, but you're not responsible for the spiritual growth of your children. God is responsible for that (see 1 Cor. 3:6). Your job is to faithfully share God's Word—to "plant" and "water." So get your kids talking about the Bible . . . and then get out of the way. Trust God to bring fruit out of your efforts.

God bless you!

# Scripture Index

# Theme Index



### Holiday-Friendly Themes

# Notes

1. Wayne Martindale and Jerry Root, *The Quotable Lewis* (Wheaton, IL: Tyndale, 1989), 89.

### Introduction

1. Allan Lazar, Dan Karlan, and Jeremy Salter, *The 101 Most Influential People Who Never Lived* (New York: Harper, 2006), 170–71.

### Section 1 Discussion Guides about the Old Testament

1. James Strong, "New Strong's Concise Dictionary of the Words in the Hebrew Bible," *The New Strong's Exhaustive Concordance of the Bible* (Nashville: Thomas Nelson, 1995, 1996), 120–21 (word 6754).

2. *Archaeological Study Bible* (Grand Rapids: Zondervan, 2005), 20, notes on Genesis 11:4.

3. Owen Collins, ed., *The Classic Bible Commentary* (Wheaton: Crossway, 1999), 19.

4. Earl Radmacher, Ronald B. Allen, and H. Wayne House, *Nelson's New Illustrated Bible Commentary* (Nashville: Thomas Nelson, 1999), 52.

5. *The Interpreter's Bible*, vol. 1 (Nashville: Abingdon Press, 1955), 979, notes on Exodus 20:1–17.

6. Walter A. Elwell, ed., *Baker Commentary on the Bible* (Grand Rapids: Baker, 1989), 54.

7. Lawrence O. Richards, ed., *The Revell Bible Dictionary* (Grand Rapids: Revell, 1990), 822.

8. Alfred J. Hoerth, *Archaeology and the Old Testament* (Grand Rapids: Baker, 1998), 208–9.

9. John H. Walton, Victor H. Matthews, and Mark W. Chavalas, *The IVP Bible Background Commentary, Old Testament* (Downers Grove, IL: InterVarsity, 2000), 172, 240.

10. Stephen M. Miller, *Who's Who and Where's Where in the Bible* (Uhrichsville, OH: Barbour, 2004), 126.

11. Walton, Matthews, Chavalas, *IVP Bible Background Commentary, Old Testament*, 277.

12. *ESV Study Bible* (Wheaton: Crossway Bibles, 2008), 517, notes on 1 Samuel 16:7.

13. Frank S. Mead, *Who's Who in the Bible* (New York: Galahad Books, 1934), 82.

14. Gien Karssen, *Her Name Is Woman*, book 1 (Colorado Springs: NavPress, 1975), 98–99.

15. Leland Ryken, James C. Wilhoit, and Tremper Longman III, eds., *Dictionary of Biblical Imagery* (Downers Grove, IL: InterVarsity Academic, 1998), 784–85.

16. Radmacher, Allen, House, *Nelson's New Illustrated Bible Commentary*, 744.

17. Richards, *Revell Bible Dictionary*, 792.

18. Elvajean Hall, *The Proverbs* (New York: Franklin Watts, Inc., 1970), 12.

19. Clyde T. Francisco, *Introducing the Old Testament*, revised edition (Nashville: Broadman, 1977), 271.

20. Radmacher, Allen, House, *Nelson's New Illustrated Bible Commentary*, 783.

21. Hoerth, *Archaeology and the Old Testament*, 370–71.

22. Eugene H. Merrill, *An Historical Survey of the Old Testament* (Phillipsburg, NJ: Presbyterian and Reformed Publishing, 1966), 303, 306.

23. Louis E. Hartman and Alexander A. Di Lella, *The Anchor Bible: The Book of Daniel* (Garden City, NY: Doubleday, 1978), 130.

24. Ibid., 160.

25. "The City of Nineveh," *ESV Study Bible* (Wheaton: Crossway Bibles, 2008), 1691.

26. Ibid., 1690, notes on Jonah 3:5, 7–8, 10.

27. "What Does God Require from Us?" *The Quest Study Bible* (Grand Rapids: Zondervan, 1994), 1284.

28. "Introduction to Nahum," *Archaeological Study Bible*, 1494–95.

29. Strong, "New Strong's Concise Dictionary of the Words in the Hebrew Bible," *The New Strong's Exhaustive Concordance of the Bible*, 81 (word 4581).

30. *Quest Study Bible*, 1293.

31. Francisco, *Introducing the Old Testament*, 221.

32. Kenneth Barker, ed., "Zechariah Introduction," *Zondervan NASB Study Bible* (Grand Rapids: Zondervan, 1999), 1331–32.

**Section 2 Discussion Guides about the New Testament**

1. *The Interpreter's Bible*, volume VII (Nashville: Abingdon Press, 1951), 257, notes on Matthew 2:2.

2. Craig A. Evans, ed., *The Bible Knowledge Background Commentary: Matthew–Luke* (Colorado Springs: Victor, 2003), 177.

3. John F. Walvoord and Roy B. Zuck, *The Bible Knowledge Commentary: New Testament* (Colorado Springs: Victor, 1983), 38.

4. Richards, *Revell Bible Dictionary*, 209.

5. *Who Was Who in the Bible* (Nashville: Thomas Nelson, 1999), 259.

6. Evans, *Bible Knowledge Background Commentary: Matthew–Luke*, 338.

7. Mark Bailey and Tom Constable, *The New Testament Explorer* (Nashville: Word, 1999), 65.

8. Ibid., 95.

9. Herschel Hobbs and the editors of *Biblical Illustrator*, *The Illustrated Life of Jesus* (Nashville: Holman Reference, 2000), 57.

10. Ibid., 58.

11. Lawrence O. Richards, *New Testament Life and Times* (Colorado Springs: Victor, 1994, 2002), 181–83.

12. Timothy Paul Jones, *Prayers Jesus Prayed* (Ann Arbor, MI: Servant Publications, 2002), 91–92.

13. Craig S. Keener, *The IVP Bible Background Commentary: New Testament* (Downers Grove, IL: InterVarsity, 1993), 278–79.

14. Clinton E. Arnold, ed., *Zondervan Illustrated Bible Backgrounds Commentary*, vol. 2 (Grand Rapids: Zondervan, 2002), 109.

15. Charles R. Swindoll, *Swindoll's New Testament Insights: Insights on John* (Grand Rapids: Zondervan, 2010), 345.

16. Clinton E. Arnold, ed., *Zondervan Illustrated Bible Backgrounds Commentary*, vol. 3 (Grand Rapids: Zondervan, 2002), 52.

17. Walvoord and Zuck, *Bible Knowledge Commentary: New Testament*, 475.

18. Craig A. Evans, ed., *The Bible Knowledge Background Commentary: Acts–Philemon* (Colorado Springs: Victor, 2004), 236.

19. Barker, "1 Corinthians Introduction," *Zondervan NASB Study Bible*, 1660.

20. Ibid., 1678, notes on 1 Corinthians 12:14–20.

21. Ryken, Wilhoit, Longman, *Dictionary of Biblical Imagery*, 365–66.

22. Lawrence O. Richards, *Expository Dictionary of Bible Words* (Grand Rapids: Regency Reference Library/Zondervan, 1985), 317–18, 320.

23. Arnold, *Zondervan Illustrated Bible Backgrounds Commentary*, vol. 3, 395.

24. Ibid., 421–22.

25. Charles R. Swindoll, *Swindoll's New Testament Insights: Insights on 1 & 2 Timothy, Titus* (Grand Rapids: Zondervan, 2010), 219–20.

26. James Strong, "New Strong's Concise Dictionary of the Words in the Greek Testament," *The New Strong's Exhaustive Concordance of the Bible* (Nashville: Thomas Nelson, 1995, 1996), 94 (word 5287).

27. Keener, *IVP Bible Background Commentary: New Testament*, 693.

28. *Who Was Who in the Bible*, 172.

29. Clinton E. Arnold, ed., *Zondervan Illustrated Bible Backgrounds Commentary*, vol. 4 (Grand Rapids: Zondervan, 2002), 202.

30. Warren W. Wiersbe, *The Bible Exposition Commentary: New Testament*, vol. 2 (Colorado Springs: Victor, 2001), 558.

31. Elwell, *Baker Commentary on the Bible*, 1190.

32. Wiersbe, *The Bible Exposition Commentary: New Testament*, vol. 2, 558.

33. Arnold, *Zondervan Illustrated Bible Backgrounds Commentary*, vol. 4, 279.

# About the Authors

**Mike Nappa** is a bestselling and award-winning author and editor of many books, ministry resources, and magazine articles. He holds a master's degree in English and a bachelor's degree in Christian education with emphasis in Bible theology. Plus, he still reads comic books just for fun, so, you know, he's got that going for him. Learn more at MikeNappa.com.

**Jill Wuellner** is senior editor of FamilyFans.com, "The Free E-Magazine for Parents"; a former education professional; and a freelance author and editor. She is also mom to two fun-loving, insatiably curious, school-aged boys.